Administrators

Supporting School Change

ROBERT WORTMAN

Stenhouse Publishers

The Galef Institute

Strategies for Teaching and Learning Professional Library

Administrators: Supporting School Change by Robert Wortman
Assessment: Continuous Learning by Lois Bridges
Creating Your Classroom Community by Lois Bridges
Drama as a Way of Knowing by Paul G. Heller
Math as a Way of Knowing by Susan Ohanian
Music as a Way of Knowing by Nick Page

Look for announcements of future titles in this series on dance, second language learners, literature, physical education, science, visual arts, and writing.

Stenhouse Publishers, 431 York Street, York, Maine 03909
The Galef Institute, 11050 Santa Monica Boulevard, Third Floor, Los Angeles, California 90025

Library of Congress Cataloging-in-Publication Data
Wortman, Robert
    Administrators : supporting school change / Robert Wortman.
       p.   cm. — (Strategies for teaching and learning professional library)
    Includes bibliographical references (p.).
    ISBN 1-57110-047-4 (alk. paper)
    1. Elementary school principals—Arizona—Tucson—Case studies.   2. School management and organization—Arizona—Tucson—Case studies.   3. Educational change—Arizona—Tucson—Case studies.   4. Educational leadership—Arizona—Tucson—Case studies.
    I. Title.   II. Series.
    LB2831.924.A6W67   1995
    371.2'012'0973—dc20   96-45748
                                                                                                                          CIP

Manufactured in the United States of America on acid-free paper
01 00 99 98 97 96 8 7 6 5 4 3 2 1

Dear Colleague,

This is an exciting time for us to be educators.

Research across disciplines informs our understanding of human learning and development. We know how to support students as active, engaged learners in our classrooms. We know how to continuously assess student learning and development to make sensitive, instructional decisions. This is the art of teaching—knowing how to respond effectively at any given moment to our students' developmental needs.

As educators, we know that learning the art of teaching takes time, practice, and lots of professional support. To that end, the Strategies for Teaching and Learning Professional Library was developed. Each book invites you to explore theory (to know why) in the context of exciting teaching strategies (to know how) connected to evaluation of your students' learning as well as your own (to know you know). In addition, you'll find in-depth information about the unique rigors and challenges of each discipline, to help you make the most of the rich learning and teaching opportunities each discipline offers.

> Use the books' *Dialogues* on your own and in the study groups to reflect upon your practices. The Dialogues invite responses to self-evaluative questions, experimentation with new instructional strategies in classrooms, and perhaps a rethinking of learning philosophy and classroom practices stimulated by new knowledge and understanding.

> *Shoptalks* offer you lively reviews of the best and latest professional literature including professional journals and associations.

> *Teacher-To-Teacher Field Notes* are full of tips and experiences from practicing educators who offer different ways of thinking about teaching practices and a wide range of classroom strategies they've found practical and successful.

As you explore and reflect on teaching and learning, we believe you'll continue to refine and extend your teaching art, and enjoy your professional life and the learning lives of your students.

Here's to the art of teaching!

Lois Bridges
Professional Development Editorial Director,
The Galef Institute

The Strategies for Teaching and Learning Professional Library is part of the Galef Institute's school reform initiative *Different Ways of Knowing*.

Different Ways of Knowing is a philosophy of education based on research in child development, cognitive theory, and multiple intelligences. It offers teachers, administrators, specialists, and other school and district educators continuing professional growth opportunities integrated with teaching and learning materials. The materials are supportive of culturally and linguistically diverse school populations and help all teachers and children to be successful. Teaching strategies focus on interdisciplinary, thematic instruction integrating history and social studies with the performing and visual arts, literature, writing, math, and science. Developed with the leadership of Senior Author Linda Adelman, *Different Ways of Knowing* has been field tested in hundreds of classrooms across the country.

For more information, write or call

The Galef Institute
11050 Santa Monica Boulevard, Third Floor, Los Angeles, California 90025
Tel 310.479.8883
Fax 310.473.9720

Strategies for Teaching and Learning Professional Library

Contributors

President
Linda Adelman

Vice President Programs and Communications
Sue Beauregard

Professional Development Editorial Director
Lois Bridges

Editor
Resa Gabe Nikol

Editorial Assistants
Elizabeth Finison, Wendy Sallin

Designers
Melvin Harris, Delfina Marquez-Noé,
Sarah McCormick, Jennifer Swan Myers,
Julie Suh

Photographers
Ted Beauregard, Dana Ross

Thanks to the kids, teachers, and staff at Borton Primary Magnet School for their continued support. They've taught me so much.   —RW

Special thanks to Andrew G. Galef and Bronya Pereira Galef for their continuing commitment to our nation's children and educators.

Contents

Chapter 1
A Day in the Life of a Principal 7
   Want to Hear a Great Story? Tips for Reading Aloud 16

Chapter 2
Principal as Change Agent 19
   My Professional Journey with One Teacher 19
   Making Conditions for Change 22

Chapter 3
Creating a School Community 31
   Goals for Our School Community 32
   Ways to Build Community 37

Chapter 4
Reaching Out to Parents 43

Chapter 5
Working for Positive Discipline 53
   The Learning Environment 53
   The Principal's Role 56

Chapter 6
Valuing Evaluation 61
   The Reflective Teacher 62
   The Aesthetic Environment 64
   The Literate Environment 64
   The Social-Emotional Environment 66
   The Instructional Environment 67
   Evaluating Students 68
   Celebrate Learning 69

Professional Bibliography 71

Children's Bibliography 73

Professional Associations and Publications 75

Chapter 1

A Day in the Life of a Principal

It's nearly impossible to describe any given day in the life of a principal to capture the spectrum of activities and interactions in which we participate. We may find ourselves quite unexpectedly involved in district meetings, major maintenance concerns, and numerous crises—from chasing down unleashed dogs on the playground to retrieving from the roof the last kickball that holds air. Still, our underlying philosophy about the purpose of education, the nature of teaching and learning, and the role of the principal guides our every action and interaction. With that in mind then, I'll describe how I organize my day to provide the time and opportunities to encourage and support a community of learners at Borton Primary Magnet School in Tucson, Arizona.

10:00 pm (the evening before)
My best days at school begin the evenings before. I try to organize my time at home so that I can take 20 to 30 minutes each evening to reflect on the day and make notes for the following day. I write "things to do" on self-stick notes that I place in my appointment book. I respond to student letters I've received through the schoolwide postal system. I also write validation notes to staff members thanking them for such special efforts as their support of colleagues or their positive interactions with students and parents.

S H O P T A L K

Heath, Shirley Brice. *Ways with Words: Language, Life, and Work in Communities and Classrooms*. New York: Cambridge University Press, 1983.

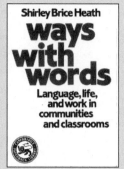

A classic ethnographic study highlighting the differences in learning styles of children from various socio-cultural backgrounds. Heath explains how children's various learning styles affect classroom learning.

6:50 am

I take 10 minutes to look over my appointment book and my notes from the evening before. I add thoughts that may have emerged during the night (usually at 3:00 am) and "walk" through the day in my head.

7:00 am

While driving my teenagers to school (yes, I do have a family life outside of school!), I remind myself to talk with my kids. I'm tempted to concentrate on my day and organize it all the way to school, but, as I strive to maintain a balance of personal, family, and professional life, I concentrate instead on my kids. We share what's going on in their school lives and in mine. Sometimes I bounce ideas off them during our half-hour commute; as Borton graduates, they don't hesitate to tell me what they think.

7:30 am

Once I hit the building, my life is not my own. Staff on the morning shift have arrived. Whenever there are adults at school, I am busy answering questions, gathering information, touching base about kids and parents, and, in general, serving as resident head cheerleader. Each individual staff member affects the interpersonal life of the school as he or she enters the building, but the tone of the day is established by the principal. The degree to which I acknowledge, greet, and positively interact with staff members at the beginning of school sets the social-emotional foundation for the day.

I follow a regular schedule of reading aloud in all the classrooms at Borton, so I pull together the children's books I am going to read for the day. I choose books that support our school's positive discipline climate or ones that will enhance the thematic projects taking place in individual classrooms.

8:00 am

I am usually able to meet with any staff members during this last half hour before the school day is underway. I schedule parent-teacher conferences, teacher-staff meetings, greet substitutes, or deal with any unresolved issues that require communication with staff.

Every Wednesday our site-based, decision-making Core Committee meets to hear reports from standing committees, share information, and delegate problem-solving responsibilities. This is a true participatory decision-making body that has had extensive training in conflict resolution and consensus building. Elected representatives from the teaching staff, the librarian and school counselor, parents, students, and hourly employees such as the food service staff and custodians meet to set goals and help direct the future of the school. Needless to say, Wednesdays are hectic!

8:20 am

If I have not yet greeted substitutes who have arrived, I try to meet with them briefly in their classrooms. I always make a point to make each one feel welcome. I remind them to read the section for substitutes in the teachers' plan books, and to review the room norms with students so that everyone will have clear, shared expectations for a successful learning day.

8:30 am

When the bell rings, I try to greet all the children as they enter the patio gates from the playground. Welcoming students with a smile, a hug, or a kind word lets them know I'm happy they are at Borton.

Field Notes: Teacher-To-Teacher

Rituals are part of every school. The trick is to capitalize on the institutional practices that are already in place and to be more deliberate about making them a focus for a celebration of learning and building community. Every school has occasion to bring the whole school together to celebrate accomplishments, listen to concerts, storytellers, and so on. We start every gathering with a song. This takes the place of nagging and shushing kids to be quiet. Afterwards I ask each class to raise their hands to acknowledge they are present. My eye contact with the group helps children know that I appreciate their presence. We always end with a formal dismissal of each classroom. This consistency allows us to create a "threshold" of entering into and leaving the celebration.

–RW

Our entire school meets each morning for a community Pledge of Allegiance and announcement time. One classroom is responsible each week for leading the school in song. This class is the first to gather and settle in with a song that the whole school knows. Singing focuses attention and quickly channels pent-up energies. The Pledge of Allegiance is next and another song (usually patriotic in nature), and adult announcements. Classes are then dismissed to their classrooms to begin their day. Our daily morning ritual takes about 15 minutes and allows us to settle in together as a community.

8:40 am

Since there are always at least 20 parents or more present during the Pledge of Allegiance, I try to greet as many as I can. I share personalized and specific comments about their children, celebrating each child's presence in our school community. It is a time when I am accessible to parents and can have those stand-up conferences that keep the principal and parents in tune with one another.

9:00 am

I read in a different classroom each morning. If there are no district meetings or emergencies requiring my attention, I am able to read one or two books I've chosen specifically for the class. I choose children's books that will help us deal with issues involving the community (such as name-calling, resolving conflicts, or sharing materials) or books that support the thematic studies of the classroom. In this way, I am in front of each classroom in an instructional, problem-solving role rather than in a traditional disciplinarian role.

S H O P T A L K

Walters, J. Donald. *The Art of Supportive Leadership*. Nevada City, California: Crystal Clarity Publishers, 1993.

Donald Walters explores the power of supportive leadership. He suggests that leadership should be defined in terms of shared accomplishments rather than personal advancement. He sets the tone for supporting school change.

Senge, Peter M. *The Fifth Discipline: The Art and Practice of the Learning Organization*. New York: Doubleday, 1994.

A well written and very accessible text on management theory with a holistic and community oriented focus. A must-read for administrators who embrace constructivist learning theory.

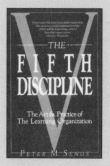

Field Notes: Teacher-To-Teacher

I never read a book cold to a group of children. I always take a few minutes to read (aloud if possible) the book to myself. This enables me to consider how to use my voice in the interpretation of the texts. I suggest you make sure you establish parameters for a read-aloud. I take the stance that when I am reading, everyone needs to be tuned-in, listening.

I prefer to have the children sitting together on the floor or with chairs pulled up together. This builds a sense of community, allows me more intimate eye contact, and means that I have more options for a soft voice when needed. Of course this depends on the physical arrangement of the room. It's always important to share books through read-alouds even if children have to remain at their desks.

–RW

9:15 am

Just as teachers like to have an uninterrupted instructional time each day, I prefer to have large chunks of time to be in classrooms. My morning time is usually spent doing a walk-about through all the classrooms of the school. Daily walk-throughs are important for me because they demonstrate to students, parents, and staff that I care about the instruction at Borton and about each student as a member of our school community.

My favorite activity is escorting visitors through the building at this time. I am able to highlight the strengths of each classroom and staff member within earshot of the staff. Overhearing the principal share wonderful things is even more encouraging than face-to-face compliments.

I usually take a minimum of 20 minutes to focus on one classroom, on a rotating basis. I have a small pad on which I note what strikes me about the classroom (the environment, interactions, activity, tone, and so forth). Later I copy the anecdotal records for my staff evaluation files and share the original with the specific staff members. In Chapter 6, I explain in detail the sorts of things I look for in classrooms.

10:30 am

I try to touch base in the office to return phone calls, meet any specific appointments, and sort through the morning's mail. This initial sorting allows me to sift through the promotional mail, and make some immediate decisions about delegating paperwork to appropriate staff members. Of course, one pile on the desk is always labeled *immediate* and another labeled *later*. I wish the two were mutually exclusive, but I end up shuffling both each day as later becomes more immediate.

S H O P T A L K

IDEAS AND INSIGHTS
LANGUAGE ARTS
IN THE ELEMENTARY SCHOOL

Watson, Dorothy, ed. *Ideas and Insights: Language Arts in the Elementary School*. Urbana, Illinois: National Council of Teachers of English, 1987.

One of the best books to offer a wide variety of ideas and strategies for integrating language arts across the curriculum, particularly in social studies and science. Teachers and administrators find this book very helpful.

11:00 am

This is my informal daily meeting time with custodians, food service staff, and monitors. It allows me to make these vital employees feel welcomed and shows that I value their presence. They are usually getting ready for the infamous daily ritual of lunch in the public school. I review plans for those children who are losing their outside time as a consequence of some behavior, or students who will be having a lunch meeting to problem solve with a former nemesis from the day before.

11:30 am

We have two overlapping lunch periods of 45 minutes each. As I make myself accessible to teachers to answer questions and get information, I try to walk through the cafeteria and around the playground. I rotate between eating in the cafeteria with each of the lunch groups and eating with staff members in the lounge. There is much sharing and community building during these informal times. I am generally on the run, making "one leg" decisions the entire time.

Each Monday, I have weekly Child Study meetings (our interdisciplinary team meetings) during lunch. Teachers and auxiliary staff volunteer for a month at a time to meet with the team to help provide support for teachers who have questions about a student's behavior or academic progress.

I usually designate one of the lunch periods on Wednesdays or Thursdays for working-lunch meetings with staff members. We meet to deal with curriculum concerns or plan for schoolwide activities or in-services.

S H O P T A L K

Language Arts. Urbana, Illinois: National Council of Teachers of English.

Language Arts has traditionally focused on classrooms and on teacher as researcher. It prompted me to reflect and grow in my own teaching, and it now provides me with new insights into supervision and curriculum development.

Young Children. Washington, DC: National Association for the Education of Young Children.

Young Children provides a variety of articles that cover the gamut of early childhood issues: nutrition, health, cognitive growth, developmentally appropriate practice, and so on. It is practical and informative.

Educational Leadership. Alexandria, Virginia: Association for Supervision and Curriculum Development.

Educational Leadership offers a variety of viewpoints regarding implementing and institutionalizing new practices in schools. The short, easy-to-read articles help me organize and articulate my own strategies for working with staff and parents.

Reading Teacher. Newark, Delaware: International Reading Association.

The *Reading Teacher* is a forum for current theory, research, and practice in literary education. It also helps me keep abreast of new children's literature.

Arithmetic Teacher. Reston, Virginia: National Council of Teachers of Mathematics.

This journal is a great guide to the dramatic changes in mathematics teaching. Our school has made math our curriculum focus for the last several years. *Arithmetic Teacher* has helped me understand mathematical thinking better, and has shown me how to explain and share instructional strategies with staff and parents.

Smithsonian. Washington, DC: Smithsonian Institution.

Smithsonian helps me to be well rounded and widely read. The articles on science, art, and history, and the biographies of great artists, inventors, and explorers have enriched both my personal and professional growth.

I also make it a practice to invite students to eat with me in my office to resolve conflicts, discuss burning issues, or just to have a comfortable sharing time.

12:45 pm

Lunch periods are over. (Phew!) I meet with the monitors to collect any behavioral notes they may have recorded during lunch. These are collected in the Discipline Log for future reference. I then meet with students who have experienced problems, or I make a note to meet with them the following day before they go to lunch.

1:00 pm

On my best days I take about 15 minutes to sit quietly at my desk, listen to classical music, and catch up on any correspondence with students, parents, or staff. For instance, I try to write a special letter to any student who becomes a new older brother or sister or has a family member who is hospitalized. Recognizing changes in the home reminds students and families that we are all connected. I always have at least one new children's book to read as my own treat for the day. I save most professional reading for home. (But I do keep current copies of journals such as *Young Children*, *Educational Leadership*, *Reading Teacher*, *Arithmetic Teacher*, and *Language Arts* in my office.)

I divide my time after lunch between reading to some classes and observing. Whenever possible, I work on staff announcements, faculty agendas, and parent newsletters. I bring my disks to classrooms, and log on to individual classroom computers. This allows me to get my planning done, and models for students the authentic ways in which I use literacy in my job. It also gives me some additional bonding time with individual students and classroom groups.

2:00 pm

Parents have arrived to pick up kindergartners and are showing up early for older students. This is a time I need to be available in the hallway or patio of the school. My afternoon availability is similar to the morning greeting time.

S H O P T A L K

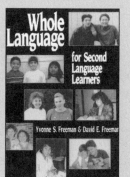

Freeman, Yvonne S. and David E. Freeman. *Whole Language for Second Language Learners*. Portsmouth, New Hampshire: Heinemann, 1992.

An exceptional resource for relating and working with students and families who are first- or second-generation immigrants. It offers strategies and ideas for collaboration and cooperation with people from a variety of national origins.

```
DIALOGUE

Obviously there is no typical day in the life of a principal. Writing
about a day in my professional life, however, brings to a more
conscious level many strategies or ideas that I have taken for
granted. Now I can examine how I might plan for more reflection
and professional interaction time with my colleagues.

What do my days look like?

_____

_____

_____

How can I build in more time for students? teachers and other col-
leagues? parents?

_____

_____
```

Since parents are often reluctant to share concerns with the principal, I approach parents and continue to build their trust. And I can say good-bye to students and let them know I care about their return the following day.

2:30 pm

All the students have gone to buses or are rushing to their extended-day classes. This is when the staff members begin to line up in the hallway to see me. Or they may leave messages if I'm meeting with parents, staff members, or attending a district meeting.

After-school time is always hectic. The hard workers on the staff who aren't "morning people" have been to the lounge to get a soft drink, and have gotten their second wind. It's not unusual to have staff members at Borton until five o'clock (even those who do not have extended-day responsibilities).

5:00 pm

This is the most productive time of my day to complete paperwork and tackle the daily mail. Most of the staff is gone so I can turn on some music and try to track the woodgrain on my desk from one side to the other. (This can happen only when the mounds of papers and telephone messages have been dealt with earlier.)

6:00 pm

I usually leave for home or prepare for biweekly PTA executive board meetings, monthly PTA membership meetings, monthly School Community Partnership committee meetings, Governing Board meetings, and monthly professional organization meetings. Or I am running off to basketball practices, games, or musical theater rehearsals and performances.

6:30 pm

On a good day I am home to start cooking dinner, and there is some daylight left to do watering or puttering in the garden.

10:00 pm

I prepare for the next day. The cycle continues.

Want To Hear a Great Story? Tips for Reading Aloud

Reading aloud to students may be the most important thing we do as educators. As one who loves to read to children and often does, I'd like to offer some helpful hints.

The power of reading aloud to children comes, in part, from your demonstration of what it means to be an efficient reader and a lover of books. So, with that in mind, choose books that are interesting and engaging to you as a reader.

Make sure the book is appropriate for the students. Chapter books don't always work for very young children, but there are beginning chapter books that are good for first and second graders. If you're reading to multiage classrooms, the older children will enable you to read books that may be a bit above the younger children. The knowledge and experience of the older children invite more sophisticated texts. Picture books are for all students from pre-kindergarten through adult. When in doubt about a particular book, check with the classroom teacher or librarian.

Before you begin reading aloud, you may want to preface the reading with an attention grabbing statement such as:

- This is a book about a boy who was so naughty that even when his mother asked him to stop, he was rude and yelled back at her. And when he was sent to his room, he began a journey to *Where the Wild Things Are*!

- Have you ever had to stay at home when your parents had to leave for a short time? This is a story of two children who were at home by themselves when a very rude visitor came to call: *The Cat in the Hat*!

- I know you have been studying birds and I found this wonderful book about eggs that reminded me that *Chickens Aren't the Only Ones* to lay eggs.

If the book is a picture book, try to hold it in your right hand (if you are right-handed) to your side so that both open pages face the children at all times. Read from the side and reach over with your left hand to turn the pages and keep the illustrations facing the children. Don't pull the book over in front of you to turn the pages as that will interrupt the flow of the text.

Powerful learning can occur when children make connections between what they know and literary experiences.

If the book is a chapter book, don't forget that children of all ages appreciate the illustrations. Before you start to read, point out that there are a few illustrations, and promise to show them as you go along. Decide together where to stop to continue reading another time. If you choose to read a chapter book, try to schedule your readings close together so that the book will be completed within a reasonable amount of time. This is quite a demand on the time you give to one classroom, but you can arrange to read on alternate weeks with other classrooms. It's best if you can read a chapter book a minimum of once daily until the book is completed.

Vary your voice to fit the mood of the text and the personality of the characters. Don't be afraid to "ham it up." The children will always be an appreciative audience. You need to show them the fun you can have with a book.

Sometimes little ones get excited and naturally begin talking about the content of the book or experiences the text or illustrations bring to mind. Powerful learning can occur when children make connections between what they know and literary experiences. Use your best judgment about when to stop the reading and invite talking. You don't want to interrupt the flow of the book, but you also don't want to lose an opportunity for learning.

You may need to move some children if there are uncooperative combinations. Usually inviting distracted children to move closer so they can see or hear better will do the trick. It allows you to break up a combination and focus children without embarrassing them in front of the class.

After reading, take a few minutes to discuss and allow children to ask questions about the book. This will give you the opportunity to revisit the text and reread for detail, as well as focus on the author's choice of words. You will build children's sense of authorship and give them ideas for their own stories.

Some of My Favorite Read-Aloud Books

Billy and the Bad Teacher by Andrew Clements. The four messages in this book are: teachers are people; each one is different; don't expect every teacher to be perfect; and look for their strengths.

I Am an Artist by Pat Lowry Collins. This story enables us to see our ability to become artists. We find that part of ourselves in different ways.

Amazing Grace by Mary Hoffman. A wonderful story about opportunity, regardless of race, creed, or gender.

The Best Christmas Pageant Ever by Barbara Robinson. The author's point is that there is a need to find something good in everyone—no matter how obnoxious he or she might be.

The True Story of the Three Little Pigs by John Scieszka. Children see that there is always another point of view.

The Cat in the Hat by Dr. Seuss. Among other virtues, the story shows what happens when you don't follow directions.

The Velveteen Rabbit by Margery Williams. The author highlights the need to be loved and cared for.

The Happy Prince by Oscar Wilde. Celebrate the power of friendship through this story.

Chapter 2

Principal as Change Agent

As principals, we participate in the professional journeys taken each school year by the staff as a whole and by individual teachers. Through daily interactions, we have many opportunities to guide our teachers' professional growth and enrich their journeys.

My Professional Journey with One Teacher

I hired Kathy Lohse to fill a second grade bilingual teaching position at Borton. She is a successful veteran teacher with a wonderful sense of integrated curriculum and project work with children.

I could have placed Lohse, a perfectly capable teacher, in a classroom where she could have shut her door and taught with an occasional comment from me. She would have come to me when she needed resources or had concerns about a parent or student. In other words, we could have operated in a traditional hierarchical principal-teacher or manager-worker mode.

But I chose, instead, to put my beliefs about teaching and learning into practice. I made a conscious decision to spotlight her strengths and to help her reflect on areas for growth. I thought that by encouraging her to share her wealth of knowledge, creative spirit, and passion for learning, she would enrich the professional community.

As I work to support teachers like Kathy Lohse, I try to put into practice my beliefs regarding constructivist learning theory. I believe that adults and children alike construct new understandings by building on prior knowledge and experience. One way we build on our knowledge and experience as teachers is through interactions with our peers—teachers modeling for one another, teachers in dialogue, teachers coaching and sharing. These interactions become the driving force that moves professional development forward, enabling us to

- celebrate the differences within the building
- build on our interests and curriculum strengths
- become experts and share expertise with other staff members.

DIALOGUE

What was something I learned to do recently? (Maybe it was learning a new word processing program, Szechuan cooking, or racquetball.)

_____

_____

What prior knowledge or experiences did I have that made the new skill easy or hard to learn?

_____

_____

Did I choose to learn on my own or with one or more partners in collaboration? Why?

_____

_____

How did I access the new information? Did I read about it, talk with an expert, watch someone else do it, roll up my sleeves and "have a go at it," or use multiple resources?

_____

_____

_____

My understanding of how human beings learn enabled me to help Kathy Lohse achieve her full potential as a professional educator. I knew from my frequent visits to her classroom that she had developed a strong writing program tied to a rich literature component. She was reluctant to share her expertise regarding writing because she was afraid that she wasn't doing it well enough and that others could do it better.

Field Notes: Teacher-To-Teacher

As a principal, I've learned to be patient. Sometimes you need to go slow to go fast!

Debra Kaplan, Principal
Jane Addams Elementary School
Lawndale, California

My goal was to help her develop confidence in sharing her knowledge and experience. Lohse was at first reluctant to host faculty meetings; yet, after several tries and with my support, she became adept at running them. I also asked Lohse to present with me and with other teachers at various district and local workshops, nudging her even further professionally.

Lohse had several outstanding student teachers. By explaining her program and discussing her thoughts with them, she refined her educational philosophy and clarified her beliefs about learning and teaching. I spotlighted her room and her instructional practices with visitors. I visited her classroom frequently and gave her specific feedback regarding her many strengths.

In our talk-over sessions at the beginning and end of each year, we discussed her professional development goals and identified math and science instruction as an area she wanted to target for expansion. I gave her my own copies of professional books and articles. I also made it a point to invite her to be on school and district committees. She was recommended to work with a doctoral student in the Language Reading and Culture Department, at the University of Arizona. Lohse and her research partner used her classroom to research children's language development in two languages.

These experiences supported Lohse's self-esteem and professional development. She now presents at state and national conferences, has been videotaped by the National Council of Teachers of Mathematics as an exemplary mathematics teacher, and is serving on a national committee that is influencing assessment practices in mathematics programs nationwide.

SHOPTALK

Cambourne, Brian. *The Whole Story: Natural Learning and the Acquisition of Literacy in the Classroom.* Sydney, Australia: Ashton-Scholastic, 1989.

Cambourne presents a view of learning and an approach to teaching literacy that liberates teachers and leads to the development of highly literate, critically aware, confident readers and writers.

Making Conditions for Change

Brian Cambourne, an Australian educator and researcher, has developed a model for language learning that I think applies to general learning for all adults and children. I use his model to help frame my decisions and interactions with faculty members as I work to support our professional growth.

Cambourne identifies these eight conditions for learning:

- immersion
- demonstration
- engagement
- expectation
- responsibility
- use
- approximation
- response

Here's how I use them to think about school change.

Immersion. Just as we immerse kids who are learning to read and write in an abundance of literacy experiences and materials—fiction and nonfiction books, newspapers, magazines, posters, labels, directions, messages, and the like—teachers must be immersed in experiences and materials that support the strategies we want them to use. Teachers and other staff members can take responsibility for sharing professional readings, engaging in professional discussions, modeling for one another, coaching, and reflecting on their new understandings.

Demonstration. Just as children need to see readers and writers using "real world" literacy such as journal and letter writing or balancing checkbooks, so teachers need to see other teachers demonstrating instructional strategies. Just reading about new strategies isn't enough. Seeing is believing. Teachers need to observe and interact with articulate professionals engaged in the strategies they would like to learn themselves.

Field Notes: Teacher-To-Teacher

The role of the principal is to support continuous staff development and offer continual encouragement. One way I do this is to provide teachers with opportunities to observe in other classrooms. Our resource teacher relieves them, or sometimes I hire subs to free them for a few hours. Spending time in each other's classrooms triggers self-reflection and professional dialogue.

Mary Maxwell, Principal
Horace Mann Elementary School
San Jose, California

At best, any outsider (including the principal) coming into a classroom can only provide a demonstration of a "canned lesson" that has been successful with other classes. I know I'm considered part of the school learning community, but I can never respond to a classroom of students as authentically as the classroom teacher who knows the individual students and their social dynamics. Teachers know this, too. They learn the most from watching colleagues teaching their own students in their own classrooms.

For this reason, it's crucial for principals to spotlight the strengths of staff members. It sends a powerful message to our colleagues when we take the time to observe them at work in their classrooms and to learn from them. Observation outside the school can be helpful, but many times outside "experts" are viewed as having a magical edge.

DIALOGUE

What is one major topic my staff has identified as interesting and worthwhile for study?

_____

What activities can my school community engage in to become immersed in the study?

_____

_____

Who are the teachers in my school who would welcome colleagues into their classrooms to observe them at work with their students?

_____

_____

What teams of teachers would naturally engage in professional interactions around common experiences?

_____

_____

Think about your major topic for a staff development meeting. Every teacher has a variety of interests and differing strengths. How can you frame the topic for study in ways that will engage all your teachers?

As principal, I work hard to help each teacher become a school "expert" in such areas as children's literature, student-generated research, math, science, and journaling. There are a variety of strategies you can use to help teachers embrace their professional expertise and promote dialogue and reflection.

- Ask them to volunteer to serve on district-level committees. Offer to attend meetings with them to help them feel comfortable.
- Encourage them to share their expertise with staff members through mini in-services at staff meetings or at full-blown workshops.
- Invite them to co-present with you or with peers at district or local conferences.

- Make arrangements to cover their classrooms so they can attend special events or conferences that will add to their knowledge base.
- Arrange to take over classrooms so teachers can observe in each other's classrooms.
- Point out specific strengths when touring visitors through classrooms.
- Arrange to cover classrooms so that you can accompany teachers to observe other teachers in other schools.
- Nominate them for an award in their specific area of expertise.
- Write about their work in the school newsletter and acknowledge them at PTA and other parent gatherings.

Dialogue helps us to engage in new learning, to reflect, and to learn.

Engagement. Just being surrounded by professional readings and seeing new strategies put to use doesn't ensure learning. As teachers are engaged in professional experiences, they need time to discuss with their peers. You can teach something "till the cows come home," but if folks don't tune in, they aren't learning. Dialogue helps us to engage in new learning, to reflect, and to learn.

Time is the greatest and most precious resource we work with in schools. There is never enough time for teachers to meet, discuss, and reflect. Teachers can get together after school, but they are often exhausted. Since I know so well the value of professional dialogue and reflection, I've developed these strategies to free teachers from their classrooms and enable them to meet together when they're fresh.

- Be ready and willing to take over classrooms when two teachers want to meet together. Read a book or have an extension activity which might involve making posters for school beautification projects, activity announcements, and the like.

- Have several good films that you can show in the library or cafeteria to two classes at a time. The film can be followed by a simple extension activity, a short walk outside, and then back inside for a story. Often another staff member will volunteer to include a teacher's class with their own for movies, speakers, or other learning events. I am not above collecting my markers for favors with district central office and curriculum support personnel to come in as guest teachers.

- Arrange to extend your school days by 15 minutes four days each week and dismiss one hour earlier one day a week for staff development. You can also extend student lunch times an additional half-hour to allow for more leisurely working lunches. I sometimes arrange for volunteer parents and others to assist on the playground by playing games and supervising students.

- Ask school resource people such as custodians, health office staff, food service staff, monitors, crossing guards, and counselors to discuss issues with groups of students. Whenever possible, I participate and use this time as an opportunity to problem solve.

DIALOGUE

How do I help teachers "see" themselves as capable and successful learners?

_____

_____

When does each teacher I work with really feel successful? How can I capitalize on that feeling?

_____

_____

How does the concept of "self-fulfilling prophecy" relate to my expectations?

_____

_____

_____

Expectation. Expect success! Teachers need to trust that you view them as smart and capable because sometimes they won't feel as confident. New learning stretches our limits. We have to visualize ourselves in the role that is expected of us before we can be comfortable in our learning. It is the principal's job to maintain high but reasonable expectations for professional growth in individual teachers. Teachers rise to the occasion when they feel that their evaluator trusts their judgment and will support them if things don't go well.

Responsibility. Teachers need to see themselves as responsible for their own learning, otherwise accountability for change will always remain with the evaluator or those who are mandating the change. You can't make people learn a new concept or strategy. They have to decide that the new idea is worthwhile and be willing to take the risks necessary to try it. Kathy Lohse gradually upped her professional expertise as she decided what new challenges to take on, experienced success with them, and moved on to even newer challenges. I supported her every step of the way, but she was responsible for her own professional path.

Use. Learners don't spend their time getting ready to learn. They are constantly learning. Teachers can read, discuss, and observe all they want, but new knowledge will only take hold when it is being used. Teachers need encouragement to risk teaching outside their comfort zone. They won't try new strategies unless they feel supported in their efforts. Principals must reflect on their role as evaluators and support teachers in their efforts to change.

Asking myself the following questions helps me to develop and maintain a good atmosphere for supporting my teachers.

- How do I encourage staff to dialogue about strategies and practices?
- Whose responsibility is it to create and maintain meaningful dialogue?
- What social and emotional conditions must be in place in our school for staff members to risk dialogue?
- What enables me to promote new ideas and practices?
- If there are any barriers keeping me from jumping in and trying things out, how can I overcome them?

Field Notes: Teacher-To-Teacher

I try to support my staff's interests and provide opportunities for them to use their ideas and test their learning. If they need training, materials, or time to pursue their efforts, I work to support that need. Mainly, I value their creativity, interest, desire to expand their professional repertoire, and evolving understanding of effective teaching practice.

Dorinda Dee, Principal
Roosevelt Elementary School
Lawndale, California

Approximation. When we try out new ideas and practices, we shouldn't always expect to get it right at first. We all have professional and instructional goals in mind, but we should view our efforts to meet our goals as approximations, not failures. Principals need to serve as staff cheerleaders and support the approximations of staff members as they attempt to make significant changes in their practices. When teachers put new practices and strategies into use they must focus on what went well and then on what they can do differently. Principals can help by encouraging teachers to reflect on their strengths and identify their needs.

Each teacher is different in terms of how much disequilibrium can be tolerated at any given time and in any given curriculum area. I equate change with the process of getting into a swimming pool:

- Some people are willing to dive right in over their head at the beginning, but come up quickly near the edge for security.

- Some people have to wade in slowly, testing the water every step of the way.
- Some need the support of a "floatie" to feel safe enough to leave the edge.
- Some won't even get into the pool until they see all the fun that others are having.
- Some won't go in because they are so fearful of the water that they need lots of coaxing and counseling before they can even consider getting wet.

Each staff member has a different tolerance for change. If we acknowledge only the divers, then we will never get the waders in past their knees. (Certainly not past their navels!) But even the divers need some help if they find themselves in over their heads. We have to support the people in the pool to show others that their efforts will be worthwhile. If the pool is too cold, full of alligators, or the swimmers are dunked too often, nobody wants to stay in the water!

It's useful to consider who the divers, waders, and watchers are on your staff. I often think about how these different folks make changes in their instructional practices and what I can do to support their attempts and approximations.

DIALOGUE

How do my words and what I notice or ignore shape the learning and teaching behaviors of my faculty?

_____

_____

How does my perception of a teacher's competency affect my response?

_____

_____

When I try a new technique, what responses do I most appreciate from my colleagues?

_____

_____

Response. As administrators, we have control over how we respond to staff members' attempts at change. We can create an atmosphere that nurtures professional growth, and we can encourage and support teachers in the change process through our words and actions. But we must first see ourselves as learners before we can be successful in the role of change agents, because only then can we appreciate the efforts and risks taken by others.

Chapter 3

Creating a School Community

P rincipals are most effective when they understand the processes of learning and have developed clear goals to support it. Indeed, a set of thoughtfully developed goals for schoolwide learning is a tool no principal will want to be without. I work hard to develop goals for the Borton learning community, and, at the beginning of each school year, I share these goals in English and Spanish with

- myself on a big chart in my office
- staff on our first day back from summer vacation
- parents in the first newsletter of the year
- the Borton community at Open House in an oral presentation (I also post the goals on a special bulletin board outside of the office area and in the high profile areas of the cafeteria and entrances to the school.)
- the Assistant Superintendent in writing at my evaluation conference.

I develop goals with input from all members of our school community.

Goals for Our School Community

A place we enjoy returning to each day. School should be the kind of place children and adults want to return to each day, captivated by the excitement and the joy of learning. The staff should enjoy their work. We encourage laughter at Borton, and try not to squelch spontaneity and fun when it occurs.

As a staff, we don't encourage parties but rather have schoolwide celebrations on the afternoons preceding holidays. At that time we sing songs we all know. Teachers plan and participate in readers' theater productions or full-blown plays for the kids. We get in one 15-minute morning rehearsal with a make-your-own-costume out of paper or anything else you can get your hands on. This models the fun we teachers have with learning and with each other.

We don't have to agree with one another to be respectful of one another.

Field Notes: Teacher-To-Teacher

Ten years ago, at the end of my first year as principal of Ganado Primary School, I was surprised to learn that some of my staff viewed me as a blue-eyed, fire-breathing dragon. I had begun the year believing that in order to be an effective administrator, I had to assert my control. Perhaps I had viewed my role as one of manager rather than as leader of others. Looking back over the past decade, I have learned some valuable lessons. I learned that I must continuously monitor my own growth, which I do primarily within the pages of a daybook. I capture not only what I think or plan but also the interesting situations in which I find myself. Within its pages, I am able to think through options or reactions to situations.

Sigmund Boloz, Principal
Ganado Primary School
Ganado, Arizona

A staff respectful and supportive of one another. We don't have to agree with one another to be respectful of one another. As a staff we went through formal conflict resolution training (as did interested parents and students). It helped us remember all the "reflective listening" and "I" message techniques we need when we discuss issues that affect the group.

Now that we are in the throes of site-based decision making as a school, we are learning about consensus building. When we vote in a traditional format we often polarize the community. Issues are seldom so cut-and-dry that a vote of yea or nay makes sense. Consensus training also helps us learn how to listen carefully to one another and reach decisions we all believe in.

We can't risk new ideas or grow in an atmosphere where staff "tattles" on one another. We can't have the third grade teachers complaining to parents or to colleagues that the second grade teachers "didn't do thus and so..." and the second grade teachers complaining to the first grade teachers, and so on down the line. Trust is basic to a collegial environment. If one teacher disagrees with the practices of another, both should be asked to explain their professional decision making. If they can't explain their practices, they should self-reflect, ask questions, read, and become more knowledgeable. The principal serves as mediator and provides a forum for exploring different points of view. The process of reflection, dialogue, and negotiation becomes even more powerful as parents begin to express their views to the staff. Our school-wide goals provide a common ground for discussion.

Field Notes: Teacher-To-Teacher

I try to provide leadership for change by staying abreast of information and knowledge relating to curriculum and learning research. I work closely with teachers on my staff who work on various curriculum committees, and I promote discussion and sharing always. I try to create a positive social-emotional tone by modeling my expectations for us to be an inviting school, one where children will want to come, parents will be proud to send their children, and we will cherish the work we do.

Dorinda Dee, Principal
Roosevelt Elementary School
Lawndale, California

When issues cannot be resolved informally, then we apply our formal resolution training which has provided us with a format for mediation. This is true for staff/staff, child/child, parent/teacher, or principal/teacher conflicts. Formal mediation rarely occurs at Borton because of the level of communication we have achieved.

As principal, I model the use of the techniques I hope others will use. If two teachers have a problem, for example, I suggest conducting an informal mediation in private. When a parent and a teacher disagree, I meet with both so that both feel they are heard. This approach also has an impact on our discipline policy. When students have a problem, they are brought together to discuss the problem and come to a solution so it won't happen again.

A modified win/win mediation. At Borton School, student mediators and adults who need support in resolving conflicts use a simplified form of a win/win mediation. It was adapted by primary students Daphne Raves and Bryan Lohse and their teacher Perry McCauley from a variety of formalized models developed primarily by the National Education Association.

In order to be the best advocates possible, the mediators are paired and spend several hours in training and role-playing. The mediation steps are printed on cards and used as prompts during the mediation process. No mediation occurs unless most parties agree. When it's available, student mediators are encouraged to use the principal's office because it lends credence to the process. If "put-downs" or other disruptive behavior interferes, mediation is terminated and the parties and their problems are referred immediately to a teacher or the principal.

Steps for Successful Mediation

1. Introduce yourself and explain what a mediator does.
2. Ask if the persons involved in the disagreement have "cooled off." If not, set a new time for mediation.
3. Go to a private place and explain that all sharing is kept confidential.
4. Teach rules—no put-downs, name-calling, or interrupting.
5. Pick a person to go first and say, "Please tell us how you remember the problem and how you feel."
6. Restate what you have heard; be sure that feelings are stated.
7. Have the second person restate what he or she heard.
8. Say to the second person, "Please tell us how you remember the problem, and how you feel."
9. Restate what you heard; be sure feelings are stated.
10. First person restates what he or she heard.
11. Ask each person to share how he or she may have contributed to the problem.
12. Ask for ideas so that the problem won't happen again. Write down the ideas.
13. Ask both individuals to choose a solution they are willing to use.
14. Validate: "You have good ideas. You sure worked hard. You were very honest. You're a good listener. You're both winners. You did a good job of solving your own problem."

A place to collaborate and solve problems together. In general, our staff meetings are held every Wednesday after school. The meeting rotates from classroom to classroom with each teacher taking responsibility for running the meeting. The agenda is put together by the office staff. Any member of the staff can request time on the agenda. The general agenda is set up as follows:

- Joys and sorrows. Our "Joys and Sorrows" at staff meetings set the tone that we care about one another as a staff. Every staff meeting begins with people volunteering their joys or sorrows for the week. It's sometimes personal and sometimes professional. We hear the joys and sorrows of our colleagues, which helps us better understand one another during hard times. When we laugh and cry together we are less likely to complain about one another when we're unhappy.

- Sharing. The host teacher shares some strategy or successful practice that worked well. Just being in one another's rooms allows everyone the opportunity to ask questions and celebrate one another's strengths. It's also an authentic reason to keep the classroom orderly and looking aesthetically pleasing because you know company's coming.

- Library update. The librarian always gets 5-10 minutes of every meeting time to introduce new books by holding them up and giving a quick "book talk." All the books are checked out on the spot by staff. Everyone is responsible for knowing our resources, which are vital to making professional decisions.

- Business. Generally most of the "administrative stuff" goes last. I still get in what needs to be shared, but that information is also in writing on the agenda. Individual teachers volunteer to take notes on an agenda for a missing colleague and then make him or her a copy.

- Announcements. Any staff member can request to have an item added to the agenda for information or discussion. It's helpful to have each individual estimate the amount of time his or her item may take.

DIALOGUE

What goals do I feel are particularly important for my school?

_____

_____

How are my colleagues' goals compatible with or different from my own?

_____

_____

Jot down a few ideas and run them by staff members you feel safe with. Listen to their responses as teachers.

Staff meetings are important for solving the day-to-day problems that come up. We also arrange for part-day or whole-day substitutes several times each year so that we can have an all staff in-service, planning, and decision-making time together. These events involve the entire staff, including custodians, monitors, and food service personnel.

Field Notes: Teacher-To-Teacher

Our staff meetings are held every Tuesday; we rotate them around four major components. The first Tuesday of the month is a business meeting. The agenda is set by the group; I collect agenda items throughout the month. Any major issues are set aside for committee work. The second Tuesday is reserved for in-service. Teachers and administrators from the district or elsewhere share information about topics such as second language learners, collaborative learning, or use of the resource room. The third Tuesday is devoted to team building, and the fourth is for opportunities that come along. An artist might come in and demonstrate the various ways to bind books, or a staff member might share what she or he learned at a recent professional conference.

Mary Maxwell, Principal
Horace Mann Elementary School
San Jose, California

Ways To Build Community

Parent corners. Parents belong in our school and in our classrooms. Every classroom at Borton has a "parent corner" where parents can have a cup of coffee or tea and are invited to sit. If they want to help, they can always mount, label, and display children's artwork. Or they might enjoy reading to, talking with, and listening to children share their stories or research. Not every parent, however, is suited for or is comfortable in the instructional role. We individualize our parent involvement to match the abilities and comfort level of parents with the needs of the school and classrooms. Every parent feels welcome in every classroom and, most importantly, feels welcome to return.

The school cafeteria. The cafeteria is often a place where children are rushed in and out. And there are often very tight schedules to deal with in large schools with strained facilities. My experience has been, however, that the ambiance of the lunchroom sets the tone for the playground as well. As children come into the cafeteria they should be greeted with smiles and made to feel that they are about to share in a family meal—not a cattle call trough experience. Self selection of where to sit (within reason) and being able to converse with friends is an important part of eating an informal meal together.

At Borton, students have potted plants that are set on the tables each day at lunch time to create a homey feel. After students turn in their lunch trays, they are given sponges to clean the area of the table where they were sitting. This is another way students take responsibility for caring for their school.

Schoolwide postal system. Borton has operated a schoolwide postal system for five years. The PTA provided mailboxes for each classroom, the library, and the office. The postal system itself is run by the second-third grade bilingual students. Each classroom has chosen a logo which is used for addressing mail for delivery (e.g., Sunshine Room, Star Room, Butterfly Room, Lion's Den). This allows the youngest children to address their letters by using their friend's names and drawings of the classroom logos. Mail is collected each morning, sorted in the classroom, and then delivered to respective rooms in the afternoon.

As principal, I receive lots of student letters. Because of this constant flow of mail, I am able to communicate with and be accessible to students. The system provides an avenue for the authentic use of the "interpersonal function

of language" (Halliday 1975). It allows me the opportunity to model writing for real purposes and build positive relationships with students. The letter writing actually happens in spurts. This is fortunate since it's my goal to respond to every letter I receive. Some weeks 30 to 40 letters arrive.

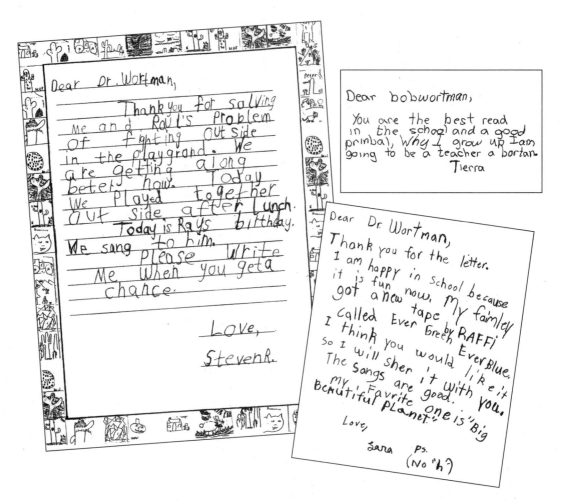

Organizing a schoolwide theme. Schoolwide themes bring the staff together in their planning, ordering of materials, and public sharing of what they have learned. In April of each year, a small committee of staff, students, and parents poll their peers for possible themes. The themes are broad enough to encompass a variety of mini-themes and tie in with curriculum goals set by the staff. The faculty agrees upon a general time period during which each classroom can focus on one aspect of the study and present their research and understandings publicly. We have found that January and February of the following year is a time when teachers can easily commit to such an undertaking.

After compiling and organizing the responses to the parent, student, and staff surveys, the committee organizes, combines and presents the list of brainstormed options to the teachers. The teachers then discuss the merits of each theme and everyone votes for their first (three points), second (two points) and third (one point) choice. The weighted scores are compiled for each theme, and the topic with the highest score is selected for the following year's theme.

Our school librarian and staff suggest possible topics within the broader theme. Resources are listed and ordered. I work with parents to identify funding sources for the books, references, artifacts, and so forth necessary to flesh-out the study. Everyone has a year to study, plan, and gather resources, making the study come alive for the school community.

Once our theme study is complete, each classroom shares their learning in some way, through plays, displays, slide shows, dioramas, and so on. In this way, people work together, share limited materials, and learn new ideas from one another.

For several years we focused on the continents Asia, Africa, and South America. During our study of Asia, one class studied tigers; other classes studied pandas; the Olympic games in Korea; the "Ring of Fire" in the Pacific Ocean; and the caste system of India as compared to segregation in the southern United States. The students compared the life and works of Mahatma Gandhi and Martin Luther King. Our next schoolwide theme was storytelling and then landmarks of the world.

The schoolwide theme this year is an ethnographic study of the Borton community. We will report our findings in a published book that we'll share with parents and the district. We are looking forward to a variety of experiences with writing across genre as well as with organizing and evaluating data.

Sing alongs. Every Tuesday afternoon, groups of three or four classrooms gather for group sing alongs. Since we have so many multiage classrooms we tend to have across-grade sing alongs. Classes learn songs that can be sung during community pledge, and kids learn to sing in groups. Students can experience singing parts and rounds, and begin learning instrumentation with large groups. It makes for a lovely sound on those afternoons.

Some of our songs come from popular music and some are traditional. All the song lyrics are written on charts; each song becomes a shared reading experience, supporting our young readers. Here are some of our favorites:

"The Eagle" by Hap Palmer

"Kookaburra" by Marion Sinclair

"The Mud Song" by Rick Charted

"Small World" by Stephen Sondheim and Jules Styne

"We Shall Overcome" by Zilphia Horton, Frank Hamilton, Guy Carawan and Pete Seeger

"I've Been Working on the Railroad" (traditional American folksong)

"De Colores" (United Farm Workers folksong)

"Yellow Submarine" by John Lennon and Paul McCartney

"We Come From the Mountains" by Bill Harley

Field Notes: Teacher-To-Teacher

When I think about an effective school learning community, these key ingredients come to mind:

- a shared vision of what is effective

- a culture and environment that invites learning

- a staff of individuals who are active enthusiastic learners

- a principal who is the leading learner

- an abundance of joy and enthusiasm about children.

Dorinda Dee, Principal
Roosevelt Elementary School
Lawndale, California

Staff study groups. Study groups are hard to initiate and often difficult to sustain, but they are one of the most rewarding activities for staff involvement. Teachers are learners at heart. They may be tired of academia and the ritualized lecture-and-write-a-paper structure of university coursework, but they are usually well-read in a variety of subjects and can contribute to the many areas of study. We have experimented with a variety of formal and informal organizational plans for study groups:

- studying over lunch as our version of a "brown bag seminar"

- having an early morning coffee group to discuss professional articles that the group chooses and reads in advance
- setting aside a number of staff meetings for the purpose of studying a topic of interest
- undertaking an in-depth, formal, long-term study group.

When the staff takes on an in-depth study, the whole school participates in choosing the topic through a survey. This year we've chosen to study Native American issues. The staff gathers articles, organizes literature study groups, and creates text sets of literature by Native American authors for adults and children. We plan to meet twice weekly over a period of eight weeks in one hour sessions before school. It's exciting to see the staff pull together resources and debate the merits of the articles and books for inclusion in the study.

Circulating fine art backpacks. We have backpacks that can be checked out for two-week periods. The students sign an agreement with parents that outlines how the materials will be cared for and used. Then the children select items such as the following for their backpacks:

- cassette tapes
- photos of composers
- portable cassette player with earphones and mini-speakers
- several books about fine arts or books that reflect fine arts ideas
- mini-sculptures that represent arts from around the world
- small art prints which have been cut out of magazines, calendars, and date books and laminated with captions on the back about the artist and work of art
- plate stands for setting up the prints as a museum
- current information from the Tucson Museum of Art and free bus passes to the museum for the family.

We also have an ethnic arts backpack program that includes Native American, African American, Latino American, and Asian American units. These are self-contained units that include everything above plus biographies of important people representing the ethnic group, traditional and contemporary music and art, and audiotape storytelling from the representative culture.

These checkout programs have been instrumental in helping us understand the diversity found in the backgrounds of members of the Borton community. Few busy parents have the time to spend checking such materials out of the public library. By making these resources readily available, we make it easy for Borton families to explore, learn about, and appreciate our diverse school community.

SHOPTALK

Peterson, Ralph. *Life in a Crowded Place: Making a Learning Community*. Portsmouth, New Hampshire: Heinemann, 1993.

This is the best book I've read on building community within classrooms and schools. Peterson explains how to involve parents and students, and details the successful strategies and practices used by educators to create and support an authentic community of learners.

Circulating take-home computers. When our district installed a new Macintosh computer lab at Borton, we took computers from the old lab and set up a take-home program for families, inviting them to check out an Apple IIe for two weeks at a time. Parents must first participate in a Saturday training (or a two-evening program or a two-morning program) to learn how to set-up and use several pieces of software. The program has helped us build computer literacy in the school and community. The students who are becoming computer literate the fastest are those students who have access to computers at home.

Chapter 4

Reaching Out to Parents

If we truly are committed to educational reform we will involve parents throughout the process. At Borton, we have expanded our notions of what parent involvement means. Traditionally we have asked parents to come to school for open house, parent conferences, fundraising, to do extra clerical work, shelve library books, or to help as teaching assistants. These are fine activities, but parents should also feel comfortable just dropping in and "hanging out" in their child's classroom. Through frequent informal opportunities for observation and dialogue, parents begin to feel ownership of the school. Here are a few strategies we employ at Borton to facilitate parent involvement:

- Welcome parents with a smile and an authentic word of welcome.
- Always thank parents for being in the school and invite them to come back.
- Help every staff member (teachers, teaching assistants, custodians, food service workers, office staff, and others) see themselves as ambassadors for the school and responsible for setting a tone of welcome for parents.
- Learn a few words of greeting and customary phrases in parents' first languages. They will appreciate your efforts.
- On every occasion you meet with parents, share something positive and specific about their child before you share any concerns.

- Return all parent phone calls the same day.
- Help office staff learn phone styles that are warm and welcoming. Remind office staff to listen to angry parents, allowing them to vent their anger before attempting to ask for particulars. All staff members need to show true concern when parents are upset.
- Make coffee or tea available for parents in a special place in a high traffic area of the building where they will see it.
- Create a special parent corner in each classroom where parents can get a cup of coffee, see posted bulletins, and so on.
- Stand in the hallway near the office or on the playground where parents pass by during, before, and after school times so you can chat informally with them.
- Include parents on every hiring committee, interview team, planning committee, facilities committee, and other decision-making bodies.
- Promote monthly "coffee with the principal" get-togethers. Invite parents into the parent room or lounge before and during the beginning of school to chat informally with you.
- Provide a variety of options for parents to participate in school. Schedule meetings at different times—during school, after school, evenings, and on Saturdays.
- Invite parents to participate in a range of school functions. Some parents will attend such activities as formal curriculum meetings, parenting classes, and substance abuse workshops. We find that holding a T-shirt painting class, craft class, or cooking activity is inviting and encourages those parents who may hesitate to attend formal meetings. It's then easy to initiate conversations about raising kids, leading to more significant and meaningful dialogue about other school and parenting issues.

Field Notes: Teacher-To-Teacher

Our parents are visible every day on our campus, and they share their voices through our PTA, School Site Council, through work on our campus, and in our classrooms. I listen to parents' concerns, elicit their help, and value their participation in their children's learning and in the adult learning we offer on campus.

Dorinda Dee, Principal
Roosevelt Elementary
Lawndale, California

Field Notes: Teacher-To-Teacher

Other principals and I have had good experiences inviting parents to informal meetings with the principal, held in the parent room, library, staff lounge, or cafeteria for coffee and a morning snack. The PTA usually helps with coffee, juice, donuts, and fruit. The experience is planned as an informal time to chat and ask questions. New kindergarten parents, especially, appreciate these coffees.

–RW

At Borton, we work hard to pull parents in and to learn from and with them. Parents feel welcome and valued because certain key components are in place.

A welcoming environment. Effective communication grows in an inviting atmosphere where parents feel welcome no matter what their previous experiences in schools. Friendly smiles, warm conversation, and a bright and beautiful physical environment help make school inviting to all. Writing and artwork are lovingly and respectfully displayed in the hallways and classrooms. And we take care to represent the work of all our children. We label every piece, enabling parents to recognize the work of their own artist or writer.

Principal accessibility. I am available to all parents at all times to make sure their concerns are heard immediately. My experience is that the longer a parent "stews" over a concern, the bigger the confrontation. I make myself accessible to parents by being present at all parent functions and being out on the school grounds at the high parent traffic times just before and after school. "Principal coffees" or other informal occasions provide additional avenues for sharing with the principal.

Phone calls home. All staff is encouraged to make every effort to contact every child's parents during the first 10 days of school to share something positive and specific about each child. This is especially necessary when teachers feel the need to contact parents about a concern. Parents need to trust that the teacher (and principal) cares about their child before they'll risk open dialogue. The key to a strong first impression is sincerity. For this reason, the sharing we do as teachers or principals works best when it's specific. General acknowledgments, no matter how glowing, are merely platitudes unless there is genuine interest and caring behind them.

Parents need to trust that the teacher (and principal) cares about their child before they'll risk open dialogue.

I recommend informal telephone calls in the evenings or over weekends. You can establish the brevity of the call with, "I was just in the middle of cooking dinner when I thought I would call and share what a delight it is to have Xavier in the class. Today, he was so helpful with a new student who started school late. He took him around the school and showed him the office and the nurse's office and cafeteria. He really was a big help and most welcoming to the new student."

Field Notes: Teacher-To-Teacher

Over the years, visiting the homes of my students has proved to be an invaluable learning experience for me. Although it takes a lot of time to arrange and conduct the visits, meeting with every student's family at home provides me with immensely helpful insights. I discover what parents' expectations and hopes are for their child's education, and what interests they have outside of school. And, equally important, my home visits tell my students and their families that I really care about them as unique and special individuals. Home visits enable me to establish a personal bond with each family.

Fay Powell, Primary Teacher
Jane Addams Elementary School
Lawndale, California

The time required for phone calls home is quite manageable. I recommend spending a few minutes on each call for a total of about twenty minutes a day. Share specifics. Be authentic. You'll find the rewards easily justify your efforts. Connecting with parents establishes teachers and the principal as real people who care about the well being of the students.

Notes home. All notes, from the classroom or office, go home on Monday. This way, parents expect notes every Monday. If they don't receive the information, then it's their job to ask their child where it is.

Newsletters. I send out a newsletter in English and Spanish every Monday. Both languages receive equal weight and are published on either side of one piece of paper. This note shares upcoming events and acknowledges the efforts of staff members, students, and parents to make Borton a better place. It's my way of maintaining communication with parents, offering tidbits of parenting advice, and sharing goals and expectations for the school.

All Borton teachers send home regular newsletters which celebrate classroom learning and inform parents about what is going on in the class. So when the child is asked, "What did you do in school today, dear?" and they answer "nothin'," the parent can say, "Well, I see in your class news that you are studying rain forests..." That's usually enough to prompt more specific information from children to let the parents know that indeed there is a lot of learning going on.

BORTON BULLETIN

Thanks to all of our parents and staff for a wonderful Cinco de Mayo fiesta! Our small school grossed $1,800. That will pay for our symphony program next year and an additional author visit.

Staff In-service: We are having one last staff in-service this Wednesday, May 12th, for staff and interested parents. It is the follow-up workshop for consensus training that will provide structure for our future site-based decision-making committee meetings. Parents are invited. There will be substitutes in classrooms.

Artist-in-Residence: A special thank you to writer Will Clipman, our artist-in-residence for the past four weeks. We are fortunate that the PTA sponsors this experience for our children and staff. We were poets—and now we know it!

Third Grade Picnic: The third graders and their teachers (and the principal) will be going to Golf-n-Stuff on Monday, May 17th. We will leave Borton at 9:30 am and return at approximately 2:00 pm. We will be using private transportation. A special thank you to the Student Council for sponsoring this special event. Please contact your child's teacher if you can help drive.

End of the Year Assembly: We will have an end of the year assembly on Tuesday, May 18th, at 1:00 pm in the cafeteria. Parents are welcome to this special program ending a terrific year. The staff will put on our annual play for the kids. This year it will be "Too Much Noise." And of course there will be music and special good-byes to our graduating third graders.

Class Placement Reminder: Your child's classroom placement for next year will be on the report card that will go home on the last day of school. We cannot guarantee a parent's first choice. Please share any specific educational concerns in writing with the placement committee. The office will be open until Tuesday, May 25th, and will reopen Monday, August 2nd. Mail will be delivered throughout the summer. All concerns will be reviewed the week prior to the beginning of school, and you will be contacted if a change is possible. Thanks for your desire to help us keep our classrooms ethnically and gender balanced.

No Extended Day on our last day of school Wednesday, May 19th. All children will need to be picked up, walked home, or leave on the early bus. Have a safe and restful summer. Keep in touch.

—**Bob Wortman**

Classroom newsletters inform parents and celebrate classroom learning.

The newsletter is especially needed to help parents understand and appreciate innovative instructional ideas and techniques. It's much easier for teachers to take risks and try new practices, when they feel as though they have the support of parents. Here is a classroom newsletter developed by teachers Teri Melendez and Graciela Ortiz.

Borton Balloon Room

TEACHERS' NEWSLETTER TO PARENTS

Teri Melendez • Graciela Ortiz

Classroom Norms

The class discussed all the things they felt were important to know and follow in a classroom. Please discuss these norms at home, as well, so that each child understands what is expected of her or him.

- Always treat people with respect.
- Ask an adult before leaving class.
- Listen to others.
- Walk in the halls, patio, and class.
- Blocks are only for building.
- Only talk to people you know.
- Tell someone when you need help or get hurt.
- Be nice to everyone.
- Be careful with others.
- Respect property.
- Help keep our classroom clean.
- Follow all school and class rules.

Parent Meeting

The majority of the slips that came back requested the 4:00 pm time. The next meeting is scheduled for September 10th, at 4:00. Please try to attend. Should you be unable to attend and have questions or concerns, we can always meet with you separately, and you can always call us at school or at home.

Voting

A nomination ballot page for parent representatives for our site-based core committee is attached to this packet. Please vote for two people.

Open House

We will have an Open House on September 15th, 6:30 pm. Carrillo's open house is this same night but will start later. If you have a child there as well, you will be able to make it both places with no time conflict. This is a time to introduce yourself to the staff at Borton and to have your child(ren) show you around the school and classroom.

Library

Every Wednesday is library day. Please make sure your child brings his or her book back by then. Your child can take out one book at a time and may not take out another book until the previous one has been returned.

Center Activities

Later this week, the children will be painting their ceramic balloons, writing in balloon journals, and making a pattern on a self designed hot air balloon.

The children will have art class for the first time with Kay Rukasin on Wednesday morning.

Señora Sofia will be starting Monday to teach Spanish. She has been in Mexico.

The children need to wear tennis shoes on Tuesdays and Thursdays for P.E.

Good news…Kathy Kreimeyer, Joel's mom, has offered to come in on Monday mornings to help with centers and other things.

Family curriculum nights. We use Family Math, Family Science, and Family Literacy nights at Borton to engage parents in constructivist learning activities, provide opportunities for informal dialogue about curriculum, and to demonstrate the power of learning together as a family. Two or more teachers plan for an evening where families can come together and have a simulated classroom experience. The teachers share the overarching goals of the program. Then parents and children participate in small-group experiences. Parents are able to experience for themselves the Borton curriculum their children are exploring daily at school. These nights also help teachers to articulate and demonstrate their knowledge.

The evenings are light-hearted and successful experiences for everyone. I encourage teachers to work collaboratively. This allows each teacher to learn from the strengths of their colleagues and lightens the workload for everyone. Sometimes a potluck dinner is planned or parents are asked to bring a dessert or snack to share. Teachers especially enjoy planning experiences that are directly related to classroom innovations that may be new to parents, such as using pattern blocks to explore tessellations or creating a picture with a partner to experience a clash of ideas and gain insight into historical conflicts.

Field Notes: Teacher-To-Teacher

Every year, our school sponsors a parent education program. Last year, parents enjoyed talks by outside experts on conflict resolution—"Children's Fights and Friendships"; sex education—"Feeling at Ease with the Birds and Bees"; and multiple ways of learning— "Multiple Intelligences: Facts and Myths." In addition, parents may join grade-level support groups that meet once a month off campus to share and discuss the concerns and joys of parenting specific-age children.

Michael Kass, Principal
Ohlone Elementary School
Palo Alto, California

Parent-Teacher Association meetings. As mentioned before, PTA meetings provide additional opportunities to meet with parents and strengthen communication. I use every PTA meeting and other parent meetings to read aloud a children's book. I always choose a book that makes a specific point. It's an enjoyable and gentle way to nudge parents to reflect on and discuss particular issues.

Greeting new kindergarten parents. I share the school goals and my views on learning and teaching with the new kindergarten parents in May, when they have their orientation before fall entrance. I share Cambourne's Conditions for Learning, and children's writing from four, five, and six year olds to better help them see learning as a continuum rather than a start/stop operation. I also explain why we choose not to segregate children by age level—why we encourage multiage groupings. In the fall we host a special kindergarten Open House. I share our philosophy, the Borton school goals, and explain that our instructional practices support our understandings of how children become lifelong learners.

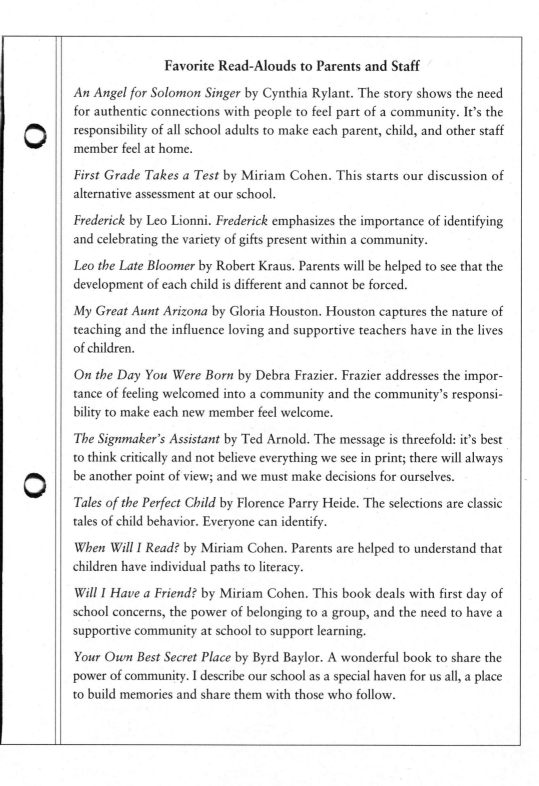

Favorite Read-Alouds to Parents and Staff

An Angel for Solomon Singer by Cynthia Rylant. The story shows the need for authentic connections with people to feel part of a community. It's the responsibility of all school adults to make each parent, child, and other staff member feel at home.

First Grade Takes a Test by Miriam Cohen. This starts our discussion of alternative assessment at our school.

Frederick by Leo Lionni. *Frederick* emphasizes the importance of identifying and celebrating the variety of gifts present within a community.

Leo the Late Bloomer by Robert Kraus. Parents will be helped to see that the development of each child is different and cannot be forced.

My Great Aunt Arizona by Gloria Houston. Houston captures the nature of teaching and the influence loving and supportive teachers have in the lives of children.

On the Day You Were Born by Debra Frazier. Frazier addresses the importance of feeling welcomed into a community and the community's responsibility to make each new member feel welcome.

The Signmaker's Assistant by Ted Arnold. The message is threefold: it's best to think critically and not believe everything we see in print; there will always be another point of view; and we must make decisions for ourselves.

Tales of the Perfect Child by Florence Parry Heide. The selections are classic tales of child behavior. Everyone can identify.

When Will I Read? by Miriam Cohen. Parents are helped to understand that children have individual paths to literacy.

Will I Have a Friend? by Miriam Cohen. This book deals with first day of school concerns, the power of belonging to a group, and the need to have a supportive community at school to support learning.

Your Own Best Secret Place by Byrd Baylor. A wonderful book to share the power of community. I describe our school as a special haven for us all, a place to build memories and share them with those who follow.

Parent-principal meetings. Most parents care deeply about their children and have every right to voice their concerns. They deserve respectful and authentic responses to their questions. Confidentiality is critical. With this in mind, I try to follow these guidelines for meetings with parents:

- I always make time for parents. I can usually judge if an appointment is possible or if I need to drop everything and meet with them.
- I greet parents with genuine interest and invite them into the privacy of my office or a meeting room.
- I usually offer them coffee or a cold drink as I would do in my own home.
- I am careful to be attentive, to maintain strong eye contact, and take notes on what they have to say. I often have to bite my lip to keep from interrupting. I always validate their feelings.
- If they are upset, I will usually ask probing questions that will help me understand what they view as the problem and what solutions they are expecting.
- I usually recap what they have stated and ask if I am understanding their concerns. I thank them for sharing and ask when would be a good time to meet again or for me to call.
- After the parents leave, I always talk to the teacher and to other parties involved and ask for their input. Every case is different, and I am not able to keep everyone happy. But I always follow-up after a meeting with a written note or phone call.

SHOPTALK

Hill, Mary. *Home: Where Reading and Writing Begin*. Portsmouth, New Hampshire: Heinemann, 1989.

Parents and teachers often ask me for books that illuminate the role of parents as the child's first teacher. Mary Hill highlights the literacy environment that children live in and discusses ways for parents to invite children to explore and reflect on their literate world. She has gentle advice for ways to read and write with children and helps parents know what to expect and how to understand their children's early literacy explorations.

Education is a shared endeavor between home and school. Borton is a successful learning community because we work hard to gain parent support. Through newsletters, parent meetings, workshops, and informal get-togethers we help parents understand our learning philosophy and how we are striving to implement it in each classroom. We welcome all kinds of parent help. We're happy to have parents assist us in any way they can—driving children on field trips, working in classrooms, or gathering materials at home for a school art project. Any level of involvement is needed and valued. The more Borton staff and parents talk and work together, the more likely we are to achieve our goal—the very best education possible for our children.

DIALOGUE

What programs are in place at my school that encourage and support our school? How well are they working? How could they be revised or restructured to be more effective?

_____

_____

Who are the people in my school and in parent groups who would help make changes happen?

_____

_____

Chapter 5

Working for Positive Discipline

Say the words "school discipline" and unhappy images of kids sitting in corners or writing endless sentences on blackboards may spring to mind. But discipline needn't be unpleasant. Indeed, discipline can become another positive component of a successful school learning community.

An Adlerian interactive model, described in Rudolph Dreikers and Vincent Soltz's *Children, the Challenge* (1964), best describes the discipline program at Borton. Within this model, behavior is viewed as purposeful. Children and adults are held accountable for their actions. The environment is structured and maintained to require students to make deliberate decisions pertaining to their learning and behavior. Being courteous and accepting responsibility for your own actions is a norm in our school community. We use the term *norm* rather than *rule*. Rules imply an authoritarian, autocratic, and top-down system. Norms imply an agreed-upon social climate.

The Learning Environment

The Borton community works together over the course of a semester to identify the components of a positive social-emotional climate. Parents, students, and staff agree that a positive climate for learning should reflect a sense of community, where children and adults take responsibility for their actions and the school community agrees on certain norms.

Field Notes: Teacher-To-Teacher

The derivation of the word "discipline" is the Latin word *discere*, signifying "to learn." At Ohlone, children are helped to learn appropriate behavior. Teacher-child and principal-child conferences, parent-teacher conferences, and peer counseling are used to help students grow in their ability to exercise self-discipline. The close, personal relationships between teacher and students result in a relaxed, productive atmosphere that is remarkably free from disruption and aggression.

Michael Kass, Principal
Ohlone Elementary School
Palo Alto, California

Sense of community. We want adults and staff to value community. Individuals become aware of the needs of others in the group and are willing to negotiate when necessary. All members of our community should show

- caring
- trust
- warmth
- decisiveness
- friendliness
- consistency
- responsibility.

Everyone takes responsibility for modeling and demonstrating these qualities in all interactions at school.

Adults have the responsibility to

- speak calmly and respectfully at all times
- be available to talk to students
- help students solve problems
- follow up and be consistent
- maintain high standards for behavior
- explain and set parameters collaboratively with students.

Students have the responsibility to

- talk over problems
- use positive phrases
- talk with an adult mediator if they are having a problem with another student or staff member
- treat adults and peers with respect at all times
- do nothing to hurt oneself, other people, or property.

Norms. The three main norms for the school are to do things that keep yourself safe, keep others safe, and keep property safe. They are worded positively because it doesn't help people to know what not to do. It does help people to know what to do. That way, whenever there is a problem, I can always ask the kids, "Was that keeping you safe?" or "Was it keeping other people safe?" or "Was it keeping property safe?" These three questions cover most of the problems that arise. Sometimes kids write letters of apology. Sometimes I invite concerned individuals to a lunch meeting. Sometimes I ask if they are willing to have the problem mediated by our trained second-third grade mediators.

It doesn't help people to know what not to do. It does help people to know what to do.

Andrew, a kindergartner, wrote letters of apology to his parents and to Richard's parents after poking his friend Richard in the neck.

per RicHaRoS. DaD aND Mator [mother]
I PoT [poked] RicHarD IN tHe Nak [neck].
Im Sare [sorry] fr [for] PotN [poking]. I wot [won't] Ou [do] it a
6ein. From ANDReW
[again]

Der MoM aND DaD
I PoT RicHraD iN tHe Nak
I Wes Sare
ANDReW

Santiago, another young student at Borton, invented his own way of writing a letter apologizing for throwing wet paper towels in the bathroom.

Helping all students know and understand the norms is one of our top priorities. Within the first hour of the first day, after classroom teachers have shown children where the girls' and boys' rooms are, they discuss the norms with their classes. Teachers share ideas about how to get along together as a family and post a copy of the norms in each of their rooms. Substitutes are asked in every plan book to review the norms with the kids at the beginning of the day and to refer to the norms when there is a problem.

DIALOGUE

What do I think about the discipline climate at my school?

_____

_____

When am I the most effective in dealing with children?

_____

_____

How can I maintain a positive climate even when children are in trouble?

_____

_____

_____

The Principal's Role

I am a problem solver, not a police officer. Going to the principal's office shouldn't be scary. It should be a pleasure for students to visit with the principal. I refuse to turn my office into a prison just because some students need a time out from their classroom. It's not my job to maintain a jail for kids. It's my job to help kids learn about getting along together.

My office is much like a teacher's classroom. It reflects my likes, interests, and my personality. I collect children's literature and stuffed animals that represent my favorite characters such as Paddington, Curious George, Lyle the Crocodile, Peter Rabbit, Max and the Wild Things, Strega Nona, and the Cat in the Hat. The kids have an open invitation to meet with me at any time. Sometimes, if emotions are high, I encourage kids to use stuffed animals to tell me what happened or how they feel. One wall of my office is covered with shelves that hold upwards of 500 children's books. These are the books that rotate in and out of my home collection. I read them in classrooms, at faculty meetings, and at parent functions.

I maintain a portion of my professional book collection in my office as well. There are approximately 300 books and my indexed journal collection of *Reading Teacher, Arithmetic Teacher, Language Arts, Educational Leadership,* and *Young Children.* Students, parents, and colleagues view me as a lover of books—both wonderful fiction and professional literature. My books are available for checkout by staff, parents, and students.

Books and discipline. Books are a powerful resource for learning in both academic and social settings. Literature is the core of our curriculum at Borton. Just as teachers read books to their students to help them deal with issues that come up in the classroom, so I read books in classrooms that will help us work through problems that come up in the school. Stories and poetry that deal with feelings, connecting to one another, handling emotions, and problem solving are my favorites. I maintain regularly scheduled read-alouds of 20 minutes to half an hour each week. It's my way of keeping tabs on the pulse of the school and the easiest way to have close contact with all the kids. In that way, too, the kids and adults see me in the role of teacher and problem solver.

Books To Support Kids

Alexander and the Terrible, Horrible, No Good, Very Bad Day by Judith Viorst. Viorst helps youngsters think of good ways to handle bad days.

Best Friends by Steven Kellogg. Kellogg tells the story of friends falling out and making up.

Friends by Henrich Heine. A story about what best friends can and can't do together.

People by Peter Spier. A story that shows people are all different from each other but still share things in common.

The Principal's New Clothes by Stephanie Calmenson. Use your head, don't try to impress others, and tell the truth are Calmenson's messages.

Where the Wild Things Are by Maurice Sendak. The message is clear. There's a time and place for running and yelling and for forgiveness.

Writing and discipline. Writing as punishment isn't consistent with the environment we want to create. I never ask a child to write over and over "I will not _____" because the message that comes across to the student is "I know that you don't like writing. You're not supposed to like writing. So I'm going to make you write as punishment." I will ask students to write as a consequence—letters of apology to friends, monitors, custodians, and parents. I will also have children write contractual agreements concerning what they are willing to do when similar situations arise in the future.

We agree to:

1. ...not say hurtful things about each other to other people
2. ...if we're upset we can stay away from each other
3. ...not bring Christina's mom into the problem
4. ...have a mediator from the Zoo Room come and help.

Maria
Crystal
Christina C

For example, students Crystal and Christina were having a problem. Crystal's feelings had been hurt and she felt that Christina's mom, a school monitor, had been favoring Christina. After talking and listening to each other, they wrote up a contract with the help of their friend Maria.

The letters I receive through the school postal system help me keep tabs on the feelings of individual students, classroom groups, and our school as a whole. I try to write to students several days after an altercation to let the students know that I'm on top of the situation, and, most importantly, to let them know that I care about how they are feeling.

Field Notes: Teacher-To-Teacher

Ohlone students are expected to conduct themselves in ways that promote safety, consideration for others, and respect for school and private property. The Student Council has written a code called "The Basic Ten" which is reviewed in each classroom in the fall.

The Basic Ten

1. Respect ourselves and each other.

2. Treat others as we would like to be treated.

3. Be caring, friendly, and nice to each other.

4. Act safely and responsibly.

5. Use common sense and make good decisions.

6. Include people in games.

7. Solve problems and talk among ourselves before we turn to an adult for help.

8. Be kind and considerate to plants and animals.

9. Respect school's and other people's property.

10. Trust our own judgment.

Adopted by Ohlone Student Council
Ohlone Elementary School
Palo Alto, California

Involving parents. We help parents become collaborators with the school. If any real change in behavior is going to occur, parents first need to trust that you care about their children. That is why it is so important to establish a positive relationship as quickly as possible. Just as I encourage teachers to contact parents during the first week of school, so I must begin to make contact with parents in positive contexts as soon as possible.

It is most important to be consistent in focusing on the school goals and norms when dealing with parents of obstreperous children. The child isn't bad. But the child may be behaving in unacceptable ways. Parents must be informed and held accountable to help make a plan with the school and support that plan. This means continuing communication from both directions. Effective communication isn't possible when parents feel defensive. My job as principal is to establish a trusting relationship.

S H O P T A L K

Children's Television Resource and Education Center. *Getting Along: A Fun-filled Set of Stories, Songs, and Activities to Help Kids Work and Play Together.* Nashville, Tennessee: Children's Television Resource and Education Center, 1988.

Remember the old Hollywood musicals like *Seven Brides for Seven Brothers* in which the characters would inexplicably burst into song? If you share with your students the tape and book kit *Getting Along: A Fun-filled Set of Stories, Songs and Activities to Help Kids Work and Play Together,* don't be surprised if they suddenly belt out a heart-rending version of "Bully, Don't You Push Me Around," or any of the other 10 great songs designed to help kids work and play together. Fourth grade teacher Elizabeth Doerr says that her students beg for this tape again and again, and sing along with it with gusto. Besides great tunes, these songs give kids strategies for working things out and can serve as openers for class discussions. In the book you'll find a range of conflict resolution activities as well as 10 stories that deal with the same issues as the songs.

Chapter 6

Valuing Evaluation

W hen you think about it, school classrooms can be quite bizarre. We put 30 children and one adult in a room all day long (often without benefit of food or water or bathroom facilities) and expect everyone to be happy as clams, to come back the next day with smiles on their faces and joy in their hearts.

And we put one "all-knowing, all-seeing, all-wise," master teacher-principal in charge of 20 to 30 of these classrooms and add on responsibilities for supervising auxiliary personnel such as food service, custodians, and traveling staff. Principals are expected to monitor and maintain the physical plant and grounds of the school and the safety and welfare of the adults, materials, and classroom pets. On top of all this responsibility, principals are accountable for supervising the assessment of students and interpreting assessments with parents and staff, evaluating teachers and staff members, and evaluating curriculum content. Hence the need to organize my priorities.

Guiding me are our schoolwide goals. As long as we stay focused on learning, then everything, including evaluation, works toward our overarching goal—the very best education possible for all our students. I spend time, then, evaluating teachers, classrooms, and programs, and working with all members of our school community to keep us on a positive learning track.

The Reflective Teacher

What makes for effective teaching? I look for teachers who love their work and love children. Effective teachers work hard to develop both their educational philosophies and their instructional programs. They understand human development, language learning, and curriculum. They are also sensitive to the social-political nature of the school community and to each individual student's unique needs and interests. Hence the need for continuous learning and professional development.

Before teachers can effectively model learning for their students, they must see themselves as learners. Teachers should be able to reflect on their strengths and identify areas in need of growth. Even though our district maintains a formal summative assessment instrument for evaluation, I strive to make the process continuous. I ask each teacher during the end of year evaluation conference to identify two or three professional goals; then I list ways to support each teacher in reaching those goals.

Before teachers can effectively model learning for their students, they must see themselves as learners.

Ms. K's Goals:

1. Continue to gain new knowledge in children's use of language and apply new writing strategies in the classroom.
2. Continue to expand the math program by integrating new math strategies.

Ms. L's Goals:

1. Take responsibility for understanding, clarifying, and remembering information communicated to me or by me.
2. Validate other staff members for their contributions to Borton.

Ms. M's Goals:

1. Continue to explore use of computers.
2. Continue to explore assessment strategies.

Bob's Goals:

1. Facilitate teacher visitation in other classrooms to gain new ideas and insights as to new strategies in literacy and math by taking over the classroom.
2. Provide access to district workshops.
3. Model writing strategies.
4. Provide professional readings.

Bob's Goals:

1. Be in the classroom more often and for longer chunks of time.
2. Maintain more frequent contact and be accessible to provide feedback.

Bob's Goals:

1. Engage in professional discussions.
2. Share readings in assessment.
3. Facilitate collaboration with other teachers to share ideas by taking over the classroom.

In the fall, I conduct talk-overs in which we discuss the goals set in the spring and decide if they are still worthy of our time and energy. I also walk through class lists with teachers and ask them to talk about each of their students. Good teaching begins with knowing your students inside-out. As each teacher and I review the class lists, we note which students are experiencing problems and may need extra help and attention. In this way, both the teacher and I become responsible for students' progress and bringing any problems to the interdisciplinary support team's attention. If a teacher can't share a lot of information about a student, then we make an appointment to meet in another week enabling the teacher to spend more time observing the child.

Field Notes: Teacher-To-Teacher

The mainstay of my evaluation process is lots of informal walk-throughs—almost daily—in classrooms, looking and observing without being intrusive. I spend a lot of time in a classroom over long periods of time to know what's really going on. As far as formal evaluation goes, I schedule two formal observations per week with two teachers. We follow a set format for the observations. They use a short form to explain in writing what lesson they want me to see. I ask them to explain what student outcomes will be; that is, what children will get out of it and what they want me to watch for. After an observation, we meet and talk. My main goal is to help teachers engage in self-analysis on specifics—I don't want to give empty praise. I ask them to write down a goal or two, and then we discuss how best their goals might be achieved. At the end of the semester, they write again about the progress they've made toward achieving their goals. I engage in this writing process with them.

Mary Maxwell, Principal
Horace Mann Elementary School
San Jose, California

As I walk through classrooms, watching teachers and students interact, I keep track mentally of multiple factors. I evaluate teachers and their classrooms from several perspectives—the aesthetic environment, literate environment, social-emotional environment, and instructional environment. I'll explain and illustrate each.

The Aesthetic Environment

I believe classrooms should be bright and inviting—clean and organized, but not sterile or empty. The classroom is akin to the family room of a home. Like a comfortable family room, the classroom should be a well-loved, well-lived-in place that reflects the full dimensions of the learning family's life together. When visitors enter the classroom, they are surrounded by attractive displays of student artwork and projects. As much as possible, the displays are created by the children with teacher assistance. Student-created displays honor and celebrate the unique children who live in the classroom.

A little clutter is fine. After all, teachers need access to materials quickly and easily, but a well placed plant or art print can hide a multitude of unsightly stacks. Teachers can add to the aesthetic appeal of a room by rotating fine art prints representing many traditional and ethnic artists and media. It's also nice to hear a variety of music in classrooms.

Like a comfortable family room, the classroom should be a well-loved, well-lived-in place that reflects the full dimensions of the learning family's life together.

If classrooms are getting too messy, it usually means that teachers are not building in sufficient clean-up time for the children. Teachers are not housekeepers of the classroom. The children need to be responsible for their own actions and their own classroom maintenance.

Since I believe the best leadership style is one of example, I remind myself to bend down and pick up trash on the playground when I walk by. I play beautiful music while working on paperwork in my office, and I take the time to put up art prints to create an inviting and beautiful place to sit and read.

The Literate Environment

Reading. Books, books, and more books—books should line the walls, fill baskets, and grace the tops of bookshelves and tables, advertising a favorite author or illustrator. The National Council of Teachers of English and the International Reading Association suggest a minimum of five books per child in any given classroom library—separate from the school library. Pleasing book displays should represent a wide range of genre—fiction, nonfiction, poetry, songs, reference, and so on. And I love to see student-published works displayed side by side with Sendak, Steig, and Seuss.

It's helpful to display text sets that bring together fiction, nonfiction, poetry and reference books related to an area of study. Visitors immediately see what the class is studying, and kids can easily access information they need for their research.

Field Notes: Teacher-To-Teacher

The principal who chooses to be a manager of programs can probably do so without entering a classroom. An instructional leader, on the other hand, accepts the idea that education is exciting, that it must be exciting for everyone involved, and that it is challenging, joyful work.

Sigmund Boloz, Principal
Ganado Primary School
Ganado, Arizona

I enjoy seeing favorite read-aloud books in attractive displays. This encourages students to go back and read their favorites over and over again. Repeat readings are especially important for struggling readers to help them build up a repertoire of comfortable texts.

At Borton, we try to keep at least one newspaper and one good encyclopedia set in every classroom. Teachers also stock their rooms with magazines, TV Guide magazines, and reviews of movies. We want kids to read for pleasure, to gather information, to answer their burning questions, and to solve problems. To encourage that immersion in print, we want our classroom walls to brim with posters, message boards, lists, directions, cartoons, and recipes.

Writing. When visitors walk into a classroom, they should know right off the bat what children are studying. Books and a variety of children's written work that reflect classroom topics of study should flood the room. A rich classroom learning environment will reflect that learning through lists of information, questions, and resources. I look for idea webs and other strategies that connect new knowledge with what the children already know. I also look for the ways in which students

can tap and share their personal funds of knowledge such as journals, learning logs, and field notes.

Just as I hope to see a lot of reading and hear a lot of talking about the reading, it's most encouraging to see adults and students writing for many purposes across genre. It's great, also, to hear animated discussions about what has been written. Whenever possible, students and classroom teachers should go public with their writing. Students can share their work with classmates, pen pals, children's magazines, their parents, and many others. Teachers, likewise, can share their work with colleagues, their friends, newspapers, magazines, and others. To have excellent writing in classrooms you need authentic audiences for the writing.

Talking. We know learning is taking place when we hear a constant "hum" of discussion throughout the day. Teachers guide lessons and whole group discussions, but effective instruction is a balance of large group, small group, and independent study opportunities for children. The classroom norms come into play here. It is the responsibility of the teacher to facilitate the classroom community and remind the students, as needed, of their agreed-upon norms. Good talking requires good listening. The classroom community is responsible for monitoring itself. Talking should be heard not just in language arts, but throughout the day as integral to all curriculum areas: science, math, health, social studies, and art.

Students and teachers alike should feel safe to try things and not succeed every time they try.

The Social-Emotional Environment

It's my job as principal to set a tone of respect, and to create an environment that fosters creativity and dialogue. Children need to be in classrooms where teachers listen to them and treat them respectfully. Students and teachers alike should feel safe to try things and not succeed every time they try. Excellence isn't in the achievement, it's in continually striving to do more.

Everyone should feel comfortable risking new challenges and trying out new ideas. A school that is a community of learners will have a spirit of camaraderie and collegiality among students and staff members. Here, Adan and Roxana give me support by letting me know how hard they think my job is.

At school, people need to feel connected and responsible for supporting one another. A *joie de vivre* permeates the school when students and teachers alike are engrossed in learning, eager to explore and share new ideas and insights.

The Instructional Environment

A content-rich curriculum invites kids to use the stuff of real learning—science, literature, mathematics, health, social studies, fine arts, and physical education along with reading, writing, talking, and listening—as tools to answer their burning questions about the world.

Field Notes: Teacher-To-Teacher

Different Ways of Knowing has fostered increased interest in an integrated curriculum which includes the arts as tools for learning. It has been especially important as a means of connecting the arts, content curriculum, staff development, and extended support for our school.

Dorinda Dee, Principal
Roosevelt Elementary School
Lawndale, California

When the curriculum is centered on real inquiry, classroom schedules necessarily change, too. Instead of breaking the school day into what Donald Graves (1991) refers to as the "cha-cha-cha" curriculum, classroom schedules reflect large blocks of time that flow from one activity to another. Inspired by the desire to find answers to their own questions, students will take the time and do the hard work required for successful research.

SHOPTALK

Harp, Bill, ed. *Assessment and Evaluation in Whole Language Programs*. Norwood, Massachusetts: Christopher-Gordon Publishers, 1991.

As our views of teaching and learning change, our evaluation practices necessarily change as well. This text opens with an overview of holistic instruction and evaluation. It continues with strategies for evaluating student learning and many practical suggestions for record-keeping and developmental progress reporting. Two chapter authors, William Bintz and Jerome Harste, suggest that assessment is most helpful as a learning tool in which students collaborate with each other to generate and answer their own questions.

Effective evaluation doesn't just measure where you are; it also reflects how far you have come.

Field Notes: Teacher-To-Teacher

If I were to give a new principal advice regarding the process of school change, I would say learn every day; value and nurture the potential in all who serve and work in your school; hold your vision of what is best for children in your mind and heart as a beacon to keep you going every day.

Dorinda Dee, Principal
Roosevelt Elementary School
Lawndale, California

Evaluating Students

There are those who will insist that evaluation can be reduced to a simplistic test and that quantifiable data can be used to compare how students and schools are faring. However, we can't assume that there is a direct one-to-one correspondence between what is taught and what is learned. Effective evaluation doesn't just measure where you are; it also reflects how far you have come. No one measure can ever provide a complete picture of how a student is doing.

We may need to produce data and use test scores to deal with the immediate pragmatics of a specific public relations situation, but test scores alone are of questionable value. Some of the highest scoring test takers in the world are in the worst classrooms. High test scores alone do not translate into good teaching or lifelong learning.

It's much more sensible to examine multiple measures that provide a rich snapshot of individual students in a variety of learning contexts. There are multiple ways of knowing. When our students have many entry points into our curriculum—linguistic and mathematical as well as the visual and performing arts—then nearly every student shines as a creative and capable learner. It is our job to provide experiences that will nurture our students' gifts.

Celebrate Learning

There will always be another book to read, new research to understand, and new ideas worth our attention. We are constantly learning. But let's remember that now is the most important time in the lives of our students. Our present actions make a difference in the lives of our students and the future of our world.

As principals, we model for students, staff, and parents that we care about the present. We take the time to meet and discuss, laugh and cry, hug and support each other in the here and now. And we celebrate learning, always. We can't discount Mondays, Fridays, days before holidays, and days after holidays. Each day is precious. Our daily interactions and activities at school reflect our view of what we believe is important in school and in life.

D I A L O G U E

What goals do I have for teacher evaluation? Do I assess teachers through informal, frequent classroom visits? through formal evaluation conferences? What practices would I like to try out?

_____

_____

_____

_____

In what ways do I support teachers in their efforts to become more effective, responsive educators? How do I nudge resistant teachers forward?

_____

_____

_____

_____

Professional Bibliography

Bridges, Lois. *Assessment: Continuous Learning*. Strategies for Teaching and Learning Professional Library, The Galef Institute. York, Maine: Stenhouse Publishers, 1995.

————. *Creating Your Classroom Community*. Strategies for Teaching and Learning Professional Library, The Galef Institute. York, Maine: Stenhouse Publishers, 1995.

Calkins, Lucy. *Living Between the Lines*. Portsmouth, New Hampshire: Heinemann, 1990.

Cambourne, Brian. *The Whole Story: Natural Learning and the Acquisition of Literacy in the Classroom*. Sydney, Australia: Ashton-Scholastic, 1989.

Children's Television Resource and Education Center. *Getting Along: A Fun-filled Set of Stories, Songs, and Activities to Help Kids Work and Play Together*. Nashville, Tennessee: Children's Television Resource and Education Center, 1988.

Dreikers, Rudolph and Vincent Soltz. *Children, the Challenge*. New York: Hawthorne Books, 1964.

Freeman, Yvonne S. and David E. Freeman. *Whole Language for Second Language Learners*. Portsmouth, New Hampshire: Heinemann, 1992.

Goodman, Kenneth, Yetta Goodman and Wendy Hood, eds. *The Whole Language Evaluation Book*. Portsmouth, New Hampshire: Heinemann, 1989.

Graves, Donald. *The Reading/Writing Teacher's Companion: Build a Literate Classroom*. Portsmouth, New Hampshire: Heinemann, 1991.

Halliday, Michael. *Learning How To Mean: Explorations in the Development of Language*. Wheeling, Illinois: Whitehall Press, 1975.

Harp, Bill, ed. *Assessment and Evaluation in Whole Language Programs*. Norwood, Massachusetts: Christopher-Gordon Publishers, 1991.

Harste, Jerome, Kathy Short and Carolyn Burke. *Creating Classrooms for Authors*. Portsmouth, New Hampshire: Heinemann, 1988.

Heath, Shirley Brice. *Ways with Words: Language, Life, and Work in Communities and Classrooms*. New York: Cambridge University Press, 1983.

Heller, Paul G. *Drama as a Way of Knowing*. Strategies for Teaching and Learning Professional Library, The Galef Institute. York, Maine: Stenhouse Publishers, 1995.

Hill, Mary. *Home: Where Reading and Writing Begin*. Portsmouth, New Hampshire: Heinemann, 1989.

Milz, Vera. *A Psycholinguistic Description of the Development of Writing in Selected First Grade Students*. Tucson, Arizona: University of Arizona, 1983.

Ohanian, Susan. *Garbage Pizza, Patchwork Quilts, and Math Magic: Stories about Teachers Who Love To Teach and Children Who Love To Learn*. New York: W. H. Freeman, 1992.

_____. *Math as a Way of Knowing*. Strategies for Teaching and Learning Professional Library, The Galef Institute. York, Maine: Stenhouse Publishers, 1995.

Page, Nick. *Music as a Way of Knowing*. Strategies for Teaching and Learning Professional Library, The Galef Institute. York, Maine: Stenhouse Publishers, 1995.

Paley, Vivian. *Wally's Stories*. Cambridge, Massachusetts: Harvard University Press, 1981.

Peterson, Ralph. *Life in a Crowded Place: Making a Learning Community* Portsmouth, New Hampshire: Heinemann, 1993.

Senge, Peter M. *The Fifth Discipline: The Art and Practice of the Learning Organization*. New York: Doubleday, 1994.

Smith, Frank. *Insult to Intelligence*. New York: Arbor House, 1986.

Walters, J. Donald. *The Art of Supportive Leadership*. Nevada City, California: Crystal Clarity Publishers, 1993.

Watson, Dorothy, ed. *Ideas and Insights: Language Arts in the Elementary School*. Urbana, Illinois: National Council of Teachers of English, 1987.

Children's Bibliography

Arnold, Ted. *The Signmaker's Assistant*. New York: Dial Books, 1992.

Baylor, Byrd. *Your Own Best Secret Place*. New York: Macmillan, 1986.

Calmenson, Stephanie. *The Principal's New Clothes*. New York: Scholastic, 1989.

Clements, Andrew. *Billy and the Bad Teacher*. Saxonville, Massachusetts: Picture Book Studio, 1992.

Cohen, Miriam. *First Grade Takes a Test*. New York: Bantam Doubleday Dell, 1980.

_____. *When Will I Read?* New York: Bantam Doubleday Dell, 1987.

_____. *Will I Have a Friend?* New York: Macmillan, 1989.

Collins, Pat Lowry. *I Am an Artist*. Brookfield, Connecticut: Millbrook Press, 1992.

Frazier, Debra. *On the Day You Were Born*. New York: Harcourt Brace, 1991.

Heide, Florence Parry. *Tales of the Perfect Child*. New York: Bantam Doubleday Dell, 1985.

Heine, Henrich. *Friends*. New York: Macmillan, 1986.

Heller, Ruth. *Chickens Aren't the Only Ones*. New York: Grosset and Dunlap, 1981.

Hoffman, Mary. *Amazing Grace*. New York: Penguin, 1991.

Houston, Gloria. *My Great Aunt Arizona*. New York: HarperCollins, 1992.

Kellogg, Steven. *Best Friends*. Garden City, New York: Doubleday, 1990.

Kraus, Robert. *Leo the Late Bloomer*. New York: Simon & Schuster, 1971.

Lionni, Leo. *Frederick*. New York: Pantheon, 1967.

Robinson, Barbara. *The Best Christmas Pageant Ever*. New York: HarperCollins, 1972.

Rylant, Cynthia. *An Angel for Solomon Singer*. New York: Orchard Books, 1992.

Scieszka, John. *The True Story of the Three Little Pigs*. New York: Viking, Penguin, 1989.

Sendak, Maurice. *Where the Wild Things Are*. New York: HarperCollins, 1963.

Spier, Peter. *People*. Garden City, New York: Doubleday, 1980.

Seuss, Dr. *The Cat in the Hat*. Boston, Massachusetts: Houghton Mifflin, 1957.

Viorst, Judith. *Alexander and the Terrible, Horrible, No Good, Very Bad Day*. New York: Atheneum, 1972.

Wilde, Oscar. *The Happy Prince*. New York: Simon & Schuster, 1989.

Williams, Margery. *The Velveteen Rabbit*. New York: Henry Holt, 1983.

Professional Associations and Publications

The American Alliance for Health, Physical
Education, Recreation, and Dance
(AAHPERD)
*Journal of Physical Education, Recreation,
and Dance*
1900 Association Drive
Reston, Virginia 22091

American Alliance for Theater and Education
(AATE)
AATE Newsletter
c/o Arizona State University Theater Department
Box 873411
Tempe, Arizona 85287

American Association for the Advancement
of Science (AAAS)
Science Magazine
1333 H Street NW
Washington, DC 20005

American Association of Colleges for Teacher
Education (AACTE)
AACTE Briefs
1 DuPont Circle NW, Suite 610
Washington, DC 20036

American Association of School Administrators
(AASA)
The School Administrator
1801 North Moore Street
Arlington, Virginia 22209

Association for Childhood Education
International (ACEI)
*Childhood Education: Infancy Through
Early Adolescence*
11141 Georgia Avenue, Suite 200
Wheaton, Maryland 20902

Association for Supervision and Curriculum
Development (ASCD)
Educational Leadership
1250 North Pitt Street
Alexandria, Virginia 22314

The Council for Exceptional Children (CEC)
Teaching Exceptional Children
1920 Association Drive
Reston, Virginia 22091

Education Theater Association (ETA)
Dramatics
3368 Central Parkway
Cincinnati, Ohio 45225

International Reading Association
(IRA)
The Reading Teacher
800 Barksdale Road
Newark, Delaware 19714

Music Educators National Conference
(MENC)
Music Educators Journal
1806 Robert Fulton Drive
Reston, Virginia 22091

National Art Education Association
(NAEA)
Art Education
1916 Association Drive
Reston, Virginia 22091

National Association for the Education
of Young Children (NAEYC)
Young Children
1509 16th Street NW
Washington, DC 20036

National Association of Elementary
School Principals (NAESP)
Communicator
1615 Duke Street
Alexandria, Virginia 22314

National Center for Restructuring
Education, Schools, and Teaching
(NCREST)
Resources for Restructuring
P.O. Box 110
Teachers College, Columbia University
New York, New York 10027

National Council for the Social Studies
(NCSS)
Social Education
Social Studies and the Young Learner
3501 Newark Street NW
Washington, DC 20016

National Council of Supervisors of
Mathematics (NCSM)
NCSM Newsletter Leadership in
Mathematics Education
P.O. Box 10667
Golden, Colorado 80401

National Council of Teachers of
English (NCTE)
Language Arts
Primary Voices K-6
1111 Kenyon Road
Urbana, Illinois 61801

National Council of Teachers of
Mathematics (NCTM)
Arithmetic Teacher
Teaching Children Mathematics
1906 Association Drive
Reston, Virginia 22091

National Dance Association
(NDA)
Spotlight on Dance
1900 Association Drive
Reston, Virginia 22091

National Science Teachers Association
(NSTA)
Science and Children
Science for Children: Resources for Teachers
1840 Wilson Boulevard
Arlington, Virginia 22201

Phi Delta Kappa
Phi Delta Kappan
408 North Union
Bloomington, Indiana 47402

Society for Research in Music Education
Journal for Research in Music Education
c/o Music Educators National Conference
1806 Robert Fulton Drive
Reston, Virginia 22091

The Southern Poverty Law Center
Teaching Tolerance
400 Washington Avenue
Montgomery, Alabama 36104

Teachers of English to Speakers of Other
Languages (TESOL)
TESOL Newsletter
1600 Cameron Street, Suite 300
Alexandria, Virginia 22314

Other titles in the
Strategies for Teaching and Learning Professional Library

Assessment Continuous Learning
Lois Bridges
1-57110-048-2   paperback

Effective teaching begins with knowing your students, and assessment is a learning tool that enables you to know them. In this book Lois Bridges gives you a wide range of teacher-developed kidwatching and assessment forms to show different ways you can reflect on children's thinking and work. She offers developmental checklists, student and child interview suggestions, guidelines for using portfolios in your classroom, rubrics, and self-evaluation profiles. Also included are Dialogues that invite reflection, Shoptalks that offer lively reviews of the best and latest professional literature, and Teacher-To-Teacher Field Notes offering tips and experiences from practicing educators.

Lois identifies five perspectives on assessment—monitoring, observing, interacting, analyzing, and reporting—to think about when designing your own assessments. As you continuously evaluate and monitor your students' learning using a variety of assessment tools, you can design instruction and create curriculum that will stretch your students' knowledge and expand their learning worlds.

Creating Your Classroom **Community**
Lois Bridges
1-57110-049-0   paperback

What do you remember of your own elementary schooling experiences? Chances are the teachers you recall are those who really knew and cared for you as an unique individual with special interests, needs, and experiences. Now, as a teacher with your own classroom and students to care for, you'll want to create a classroom environment that supports each student as an individual while drawing the class together as a thriving learning community.

Lois Bridges offers you the basics of effective elementary school teaching: how to construct a curriculum that focuses not only on what you will teach but how you will teach and evaluate it; how to build a sense of community and responsibility among your students; and how to organize your classroom to support learning and to draw on learning resources from parents and the larger community beyond school.

Drama as a Way of Knowing
Paul G. Heller
1-57110-050-4   paperback

Paul Heller is an experienced teacher, playwright, and producer who is passionate about communicating through language, drama, and music. In this engaging book he shows you how to use drama as an effective part of all classroom learning. While making it clear you don't need previous dramatic training or experience, he presents the nuts and bolts of pantomime and improvisation, of writing and acting scenes, even creating and presenting large-scale productions.

Through his Ten-Step Process in which you, the teacher, are the director, he shows what you should do to guide your students through rewarding dramatic experiences. You will see that drama is a wonderful learning tool that enables students to explore multiple dimensions of their thinking and understanding. And not only is drama academically rewarding and beneficial, it's great fun as well!

Math as a Way of Knowing
Susan Ohanian
1-57110-051-2   paperback

Award-winning author Susan Ohanian conducts a lively tour of classrooms around the country where "math time" means stimulating learning experiences. To demonstrate the point that mathematics is an active, ongoing way of perceiving and interacting with the world, she explores teaching mathematical concepts through hands-on activities; writing and talking about what numbers mean; discovering the where and why of math in everyday life; finding that there are often multiple ways to solve the same problem.

Focusing on the NCTM's *Curriculum and Evaluation Standards for School Mathematics*, Susan takes you into classrooms for a firsthand look at exciting ways the standards are implemented through innovative practices. She introduces you to new ways to organize your curriculum and classroom; suggests ways to create meaningful mathematics homework; gives you ideas to connect math across the curriculum; and links the reflective power of writing to support mathematical understanding.

For the nonspecialist in particular, Susan shows that math really is an exciting and powerful tool that students can really understand and apply in their lives.

Music as a Way of Knowing
Nick Page
1-57110-052-0   paperback

Nick Page loves to make and share music with his students, and it's likely that you will too by the time you've finished his passionate, thought-provoking book. You will also have developed a new understanding of and appreciation for the role music can play in supporting learners.

Rich with ideas on how to use music in the classroom, *Music as a Way of Knowing* will appeal especially to classroom teachers who are not musicians, but who enjoy and learn from music and want to use it with their students. Nick provides simple instructions for writing songs, using music to support learning across the curriculum, teaching singing effectively, and identifying good songs to use in the classroom.

He assures you that with time, all students can sing well. And once you've read this book, you'll have the confidence to trust yourself and your students to sing and learn well through the joy and power of music.